HANSONS
FIRST
MARATHON

HANSONS
FIRST
MARATHON

STEP UP TO 26.2 THE HANSONS WAY

Luke Humphrey with Keith and Kevin Hanson

Boulder, Colorado

▼velopress®

3002 Sterling Circle, Suite 100
Boulder, Colorado 80301–2338 USA

VeloPress is the leading publisher of books on endurance sports and is a division of Pocket Outdoor Media. Focused on cycling, triathlon, running, swimming, and nutrition/diet, VeloPress books help athletes achieve their goals of going faster and farther. Preview books and contact us at velopress.com.

Distributed in the United States and Canada by Ingram Publisher Services

Library of Congress Cataloging-in-Publication Data

Names: Humphrey, Luke, 1981- author. | Hanson, Keith, author. | Hanson, Kevin, author.
Title: Hansons first marathon: step up to 26.2 the Hansons way / Luke Humphrey with Keith and Kevin Hanson.
Description: Boulder, Colorado: VeloPress, [2018] | Includes bibliographical references and index.
Identifiers: LCCN 2018030678 (print) | LCCN 2018032735 (ebook) | ISBN 9781937716950 | ISBN 9781937715793 (pbk.: alk. paper)
Subjects: LCSH: Marathon running—Training.
Classification: LCC GV1065.17.T73 (ebook) | LCC GV1065.17.T73 H855 2018 (print) | DDC 796.42/52—dc23
LC record available at https:lccn.loc.gov/2018030678

This paper meets the requirements of ANSI/NISO Z39.48-1992 (Permanence of Paper).

Cover design by Pete Garceau
Cover photograph courtesy of MarathonFoto
Interior design by Megan Roy
Illustrations by Charlie Layton

18   19   20 / 10   9   8   7   6   5   4   3   2   1

CONTENTS

Introduction

There's no denying the mystique of the marathon. For many, it is the quintessential endurance event, at the top of bucket lists, running résumés, and lifetime achievement goals. Whatever your pace or finishing time, crossing the finish line of your first marathon can be as much a spiritual experience as a physical one, providing you with a profound sense of meaning, pride, and accomplishment. Despite all manner of newfangled endurance events popping up on race calendars each year, from Spartan races to zombie runs, the marathon remains the gold standard for human-powered locomotion. Entertaining the thought of running 26.2 miles on foot may scare the daylights out of you. Questions abound: Can I really run that far? How do I begin to train for something like that? Will it hurt? What if I fail?

Hopefully among those contemplations of self-doubt shine rays of hope and excitement. That's how Big Goals work—they seem just outside our reach, which is precisely what makes them so alluring. The gravitational pull of the marathon is very strong for some of us. For others, it holds a spot in the "maybe someday" category—a goal that you'd like to tackle at some point, but just haven't yet found the time. If you're in that camp, the fact that you've picked up this book is a good sign that "someday" is a lot closer than you thought.

You certainly won't be alone. The marathon's growing popularity has ushered in an ever-burgeoning number of participants. Today's marathon start lines are populated by all types of runners: hard-core veterans, yes, but also soccer moms and dads, fund-raisers, harriers, and weekend warriors—all on a mission to prove to themselves that they can do it. And guess what: They can. And so can you.

Most of us just need a place to start—terra firma from which to make that initial leap into training for the 26.2-mile distance—and confidence about where we're headed. That's what this book is all about.

Who Should Run a Marathon?

When brothers Keith and Kevin Hanson, coaches and co-founders of the elite Hansons-Brooks Distance Project, first devised their marathon training plans back in 1991, the marathon scene looked dramatically different than it does today. Charity fund-raising for events was but a blip on the radar. Themed races were inconceivable. Carbo-loading involved strictly white pasta and bread. Running shoes were heavier. And moisture-wicking finisher T-shirts weren't even a glimmer in the most experienced runner's eye.

Statistics culled by Running USA provide an interesting window into how the marathon scene has evolved over the past several decades. For instance, in 1980, roughly 143,000 people ran a marathon. The majority of those runners were between 20 and 39 years old, and just 10 percent were women. By 1995, about the time the Hanson brothers penned their first Marathon Method schedules, those numbers had grown a bit. That year there were about 293,000 marathon finishers. The number of women participants had grown to 26 percent, and the number of runners in the masters category (age 40 and up) increased from 26 percent of the marathon running population in 1980 to 41 percent. By 2015, the marathon boasted more than 500,000 finishers for the previous two years, and has remained at that level since. The number of women participants nearly equals the number of men, and masters runners make up almost half of all finishers.

In addition to a wider demographic, the statistics show that overall pace has also changed dramatically. Today's marathoners are slower on average. In 1980, the average time for women was 4:02 and for men 3:32. By 1995, those numbers had slowed to 4:15 and 3:54 respectively and by 2015, we had become a nation of 4-hour marathoners, with women averaging 4:45 and men 4:20.

What do all these stats say about running marathons today? Prior to the first running boom in the 1970s, the runners who made up that small group of marathoners could only be described as hard-core. It was an insular group, logging many miles in solitary pursuit of their training goals. Back then, most people probably didn't know anyone who had run—or even had ambitions to run—a marathon.

Nowadays, there are not only thousands of additional races from which to choose, but also these races are billed as grand events. These aren't your grandpa's races, with 20 people racing each other sans water stops and fueling stations. Many marathons are extravagant affairs that garner millions in charity dollars and other revenue. The loneliness of the long-distance runner has made way for the nation's most well-attended social club. And while there remain some "purists" who scoff at these developments, we would argue that the sport is better for it. The marathon is more inclusive and accessible, inviting a new generation of people to participate in an activity that has proven benefits for both body and mind. In the end, that's a good result for everyone involved. As the saying goes, "a rising tide raises all boats" whether your destination is a fund-raising goal, a personal best, or an Olympic berth.

The primary aim of this book is to show you that, regardless of experience, finishing a marathon is something just about anyone can accomplish. In these pages, you will learn how to do more than simply survive your first marathon and check it off the list. Rather, you will learn how to thrive, by not only learning best training practices, but also knowing what to anticipate during the process.

Along with detailed explanations of why and how to log mileage and properly structure your training, we will dispel common myths and misconceptions and chart a course for a successful finish. We've also polled experienced athletes on what they wish they had known leading up to their own first marathons in order to offer you the benefit of learning from others' mistakes and triumphs.

Where Is My Starting Line?

Who will benefit from reading this book? The short answer is anyone who is looking to run that first marathon. In most cases, you will fall into one of three categories.

The Beginner: Perhaps you've long contemplated taking up running or maybe you've had a sudden spark of insight or a life-changing event, but you have decided that now is the time to take charge and knock off that big bucket list item: the marathon. If you fall into this category, you probably don't have a lot of stored knowledge on best training practices. You may run the odd day during the workweek or on the weekend, but not consistently or with any structure. This book can be a key part of your journey from 0.0 to 26.2—and if the process turns a bucket list item into a lifelong passion, all the better.

The Recreational Runner: You're in the largest group of marathon first-timers. Your typical training includes 2–4 days of running per week and you are familiar with terms like "intervals," "repeats," or "tempo runs." You probably have some 5K and 10K races under your belt and maybe a few half-marathons. Many runners in this category started running for health and fitness, but continued because they enjoyed the sport and competition. If you find yourself in this crowd, this book will show you how to safely and effectively structure your training in order to take that next step on your running journey.

The Competitive Runner: You've logged some impressive personal bests and may even be the top finisher at your local 5K and 10K races, and now you're looking for a new dragon to slay. The marathon is a race that many competitive runners feel a strong pull to attempt at least once, even if they tend to prefer shorter-distance racing. This book will help you bridge the gap between fast racing at shorter distances and proper pacing at the 26.2-mile event.

If Only I Had Known . . .

We have personally coached hundreds of runners through the years, and been introduced to tens of thousands more across a wide spectrum of ability and experience through our books. So we had a large pool from which to draw when we decided to poll athletes about their first-time marathon experiences. What went well? What were the surprises, both good and bad, along the way? What do they wish they had known before they started training? As we collected responses, we noticed a number of common revelations.

The marathon is hard: Many wished they had recognized earlier how challenging the marathon was going to be—and how different the training was from 5K and 10K training. Any coach who tells you that you can train minimally and be successful at the marathon distance is doing you a disservice. The marathon is hard and you need to prepare for that, not just physically, but mentally.

Haphazard training doesn't work: Runners who didn't follow a structured training plan for their first marathon wished they had. A number of runners simply winged it on their first attempt, working off scattershot advice from friends or a simplified plan from the Internet. As with most things, they ended up getting what they paid for. Following a sound, vetted plan that explains the reasoning behind your training, as well as options for individualization, is key to your marathon success.

Marathon training is time consuming: The vast majority of runners surveyed said they wished they had anticipated the significant time commitment that would be required. Think of it this way: While you may have trained for a 5K race before, a marathon is roughly eight times as long. While it won't take eight times the time commitment, believing that you won't need to clear additional time will certainly lead to frustration. Not only is this important in terms of anticipating priorities, it's also vital to set realistic expectations for your family and friends.

IN OTHER WORDS

"The biggest lesson I learned is that willpower alone won't get the job done. Performing well requires a respect for nutrition, body mechanics/ stretching, equipment, and a host of other small details."
—David H.

"Taking pleasure in the process is really important.
If you take pride in your training and your discipline, and trust the plan you are following, the race will take care of itself. And it will feel like a real reward, rather than something you have to endure."
—Gildas B.

"I have two phases of my life … the person before October 18, 2008 [the date of my first marathon] and the one after. Once I completed the race, I decided that I did not want to go back to being the person that I was before I started running. I feel better, I eat better, my mental outlook is better, my blood pressure is better, and I have more energy. It is never too late to start and it is all possible."

—Craig B.

It was all worth it: Proving to themselves that they were capable of conquering the challenge was a fair trade for the sacrifice and hard work they put in. In fact, the majority of the athletes we spoke to have gone from simply wanting to finish their first marathon to becoming veterans at the distance.

Where Do I Go from Here?

So how do we get from point A to point B—from a desire to run a marathon to crossing the finish line? This book poses several questions to ask yourself before you lace up and head out the door. Your answers will guide you in your initial stages of training, helping you determine things like how long it will take to build fitness appropriate for marathon training and how ready you are to start training today. We will also discuss how to balance ambitions with reality in goal setting, as well as how to stay motivated throughout training. Taking the time to first establish these components will put you in the best position to begin your marathon training.

Let's get started!

Before You Begin

1

ESTABLISHING YOUR STARTING POINT

THE GUIDANCE IN THIS BOOK is the culmination of thousands of hours Hansons coaches have spent working with runners over the years and what we have figured out together along the way. My own academic background in exercise physiology is important, but there's truly no substitute for real work with runners out on the roads and trails. While we might not be able to actually sit down with you prior to your own marathon buildup, we hope to guide you in the same way we do the athletes with whom we work face to face. That guidance begins with the simple questions we ask every athlete we coach.

5 Questions to Ask Before You Start Training

While there is no such thing as a one-size-fits-all training plan, there are several questions you should ask yourself to ensure a greater chance of success. Ask yourself the following questions prior to beginning your marathon training in order to help guide yourself toward the smartest way forward.

Question 1. Am I running on a regular basis?

Runners generally answer this one of three ways.

No. I'm new to running.

If this is you, the first order of business is to get yourself up and running. Your smartest, safest approach will be to first take the time to build your strength and endurance. You can do so by starting your training with our "Couch to Marathon" (C2THON) program, designed for brand-new runners. The plan, laid out in Chapter 7, first takes you through an 8-week training regimen that is aimed at slowly and safely building your mileage and fitness from scratch. This first section of the C2THON program is our "0 to 5K" (0–5K) plan. It includes a run/walk progression to help you work your way up to 30 minutes or more of continuous running.

As a new runner, it is important that you allot time for this safe buildup prior to jumping into marathon training. What does this mean as far as timing? When you combine our 8-week 0–5K plan with an 18- to 20-week marathon plan, you're looking at 26 to 30 weeks of structured training. This may sound like a lot, but it ends up far more time-efficient than if you were to go directly into marathon training, get injured, spend time recovering, and then start over. So do yourself a favor—put in the early work to ensure a solid foundation and a smoother training experience. Once you've put the work in, you can then pick up the From Scratch or Just Finish Plan.

No. I used to run regularly, but injuries/illness forced me to take time off.

If this is you, just bouncing back from a period of time away from running, we strongly advise you delay your comeback until your body is fully ready. Injured runners often get overzealous in their return to training and as a result, end up taking two steps back for every step forward. Not only should you be confident that you're healthy and recovered before you start training, it's also important that you identify whatever it was that put you on the bench in the first place. Were you running too many miles? Do you have a strength imbalance? Was it an old injury rearing its ugly head? Whatever it may be, address the issue so it doesn't come back to haunt you during marathon training. While you don't need to ease in with a 0–5K program, be sure to log at least a few weeks of easy mileage before beginning regular marathon training.

Yes. I run several days a week and have been doing so for a number of months or years.

If this is your answer, you are most likely ready to jump into marathon training immediately. If you are handling at least 15 miles per week and you have 18–20 weeks to devote to your marathon buildup, you're in business.

Question 2. Have I run any races recently?

A few years ago, I was asked by the American Cancer Society to help people train for Detroit's biggest marathon. I quickly realized that some of these folks had never run a race—of any distance—before. This was problematic for me as a coach because, without a recent race time, I had little to go on to determine a runner's fitness, and thereby, an informed starting point for his or her training. Just about any race distance can be plugged into a race equivalency calculator and it will give you equal performances at other distances. If you recently ran a 5K in 25 minutes, for instance, the Hansons Race Equivalency Calculator predicts you could run a marathon in just under four hours. (You will find a comprehensive interactive calculator online at Hansons Coaching, or refer to the chart in Chapter 9.)

Having real data from a recent race to inform your goal setting is extremely helpful. However, if you do not have that data, fear not. You have a few options. You can launch into your training by running a local 5K or 10K to gauge your current fitness; races are fairly easy to find on any given weekend. If you don't want to jump right into a race, that is OK too. It just means that the first several weeks of training will be a bit of a guessing game in terms of establishing paces, and it may necessitate tacking on several extra weeks to the beginning of the schedule to determine where you are. As your training progresses, it makes sense to sign up for a shorter race or two to test your fitness and help you pinpoint a marathon time goal.

If you do have some recent shorter races under your belt, then you have much of the information you need to set an appropriate marathon goal. We will discuss in more detail how to best utilize the race equivalency method and apply it to goal setting in Chapter 9.

Question 3. Why do you want to do a marathon?

Marathon training is a significant undertaking. And a lengthy one. In order to stay motivated, it's important to know why you're doing what you're doing. When you ask yourself, *What do I want to get out of this experience?*, you should have an answer (or answers) to that question.

Runners respond to this question in a variety of ways. Some are looking for a lifestyle overhaul, and taking on the challenge of a marathon feels like a good way to jump-start that process. Others are driven by some kind of competitive goal, such as qualifying for the Boston Marathon. Some are drawn by the allure of the bucket list. These are all perfectly valid reasons to take on the marathon distance. Where you might run into trouble is if you see yourself in either of the following descriptions.

No goal: The lack of an identifiable goal can undermine your training. The marathon is a long-term undertaking and without a guiding goal, you're less likely to stick with the plan. Some runners—new ones in particular—are hesitant to set a goal because a part of them doubts they can do it. If this sounds like you, consider first taking on the 0–5K plan. We've had a number of athletes over the years who were unable to verbalize a marathon goal until they got started in a 5K training program. With time and miles, they started building a base of confidence, which allowed them to identify a goal and purpose beyond "just finishing" a marathon.

Goal without commitment: You have big goals, but you don't have the time or motivation to train adequately. I want to be brutally honest: Training for a marathon is hard, whether it is a 5-hour marathon, a 4-hour marathon, or a 3-hour marathon. No matter what numbers you'd like to see on the clock as you cross the finish line, training requires day-in and day-out commitment and effort. What's more, the faster you get, the more training you have to put in to continue to see progress. Lofty goals will require more mileage, harder workouts, and a greater amount of recovery. If you aren't realistic about this and you set a goal that requires more time and effort than you're able to put in, you're likely to flounder. It's good to be confident and optimistic about your goals, but also be sure to be reasonable.

Question 4. How much time can you dedicate to marathon training?

There's no way around it: There are only 24 hours in a day and 168 hours in a week. Marathon training is going to require a good chunk of those hours. Before you sign on the dotted line of the race registration form, consider whether now is the right time to make training the priority it needs to be. Remember, training will probably involve some compromise in other areas of your life. For example, it might mean that you skip watching Saturday morning cartoons with your kids so you can get in your long run. Or that you decide to shelve that home-improvement project or delay taking on that new responsibility at work.

It is difficult to adhere 100 percent to a training schedule. Some flexibility is required. However, while we all have days when we fall off the training wagon, if you are able to complete only, say, 70 percent of a program, it isn't going to help you successfully finish a marathon and achieve your goals. It's all about sitting down and deciding what you really need and want out of life. If running a marathon is part of that vision, you'll find a way to make training a priority. But if now isn't a good time to carve out that space, you might determine it is more reasonable to take a crack at it down the road. Step back, assess the larger landscape of your life, and envision where training will fit into the topography. It may require significant changes or shifts in your daily schedule. Or perhaps you will find that simply becoming more efficient in other areas opens up the time you need to train.

Keep in mind that all training days are not created equal. With our system, there are typically 2–3 days in the week that require a fair amount of time for training. On other days, the time commitment is less. In terms of overall time commitment, you can expect training to take about 10–12 hours per week at the peak of training. Ask yourself, Do I realistically have that time to devote to the marathon?

Question 5. Are you injury prone?

Consider carefully before you answer that. Many athletes we coach initially tell us that they can't run high mileage because they have found that they get injured easily. We've discovered, however, that many of these folks aren't all that injury-prone when they are subscribing to a smart, quality training plan. Some simply haven't been taught how to safely and effectively approach a running program. Others aren't sure how to tell the difference between the discomfort that inherently accompanies training and an ache that signals injury and requires medical attention. That said, some runners truly are injury-prone. Past injuries, physiological quirks (such as leg-length discrepancies), and other factors can predispose certain runners to spending more time on the bench. We will revisit this topic in greater depth in

Chapter 5, but for now, simply keep in mind a few common root causes of running injuries.

Inconsistent training: We don't expect you to do every single workout and run every single mile in our plans. The reality is, life happens. Kids get sick, work schedules change, and cars unexpectedly break down. Sometimes the sun, earth, moon, and stars just don't come into alignment when you need them to. To assure success, however, you will need to do the large majority of the workouts. If you can be consistent and gradually increase your training capacity, then you'll not only run faster, but you'll also build the fitness necessary to avoid common training injuries. Missing several days of training and then trying to play catch-up by piling on the miles almost always results in injury and illness. Remember, slow and steady wins the race when we are talking about the larger picture of training.

A mix-and-match approach to training: Some runners attempt their first marathon by piecing together a plan from various bits of advice they've garnered from the Internet and suggestions from friends. The problem with this approach is that the training consists only of what the runner wants to do, rather than what he or she needs to do. This can not only thwart your goal time, but also upset the proper balance of training and cause injury. The Hansons training plans endeavor to keep you from falling victim to the less-than-satisfying results that such a haphazard approach to training can produce.

Previous injuries and ailments: Whether you're an experienced runner or a complete novice, if you've had chronic injuries, it's important to get clearance from your physician before starting to train for a marathon. He or she may suggest that you keep your running mileage low and gain fitness through other means—something that certainly can be accommodated (see the section

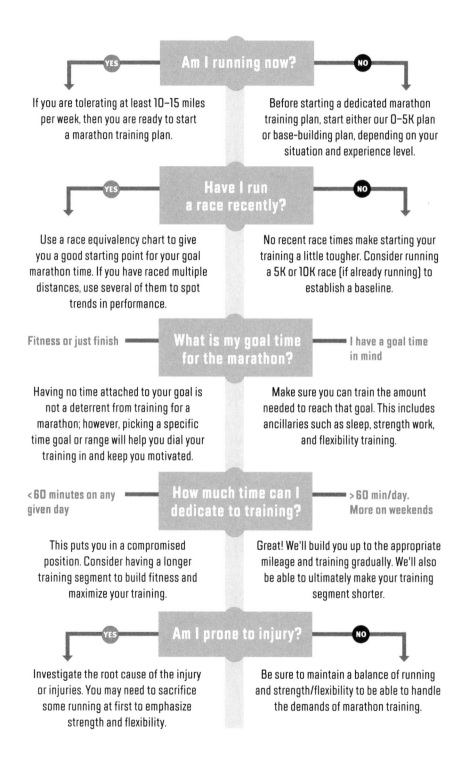

Am I running now?

YES: If you are tolerating at least 10–15 miles per week, then you are ready to start a marathon training plan.

NO: Before starting a dedicated marathon training plan, start either our 0–5K plan or base-building plan, depending on your situation and experience level.

Have I run a race recently?

YES: Use a race equivalency chart to give you a good starting point for your goal marathon time. If you have raced multiple distances, use several of them to spot trends in performance.

NO: No recent race times make starting your training a little tougher. Consider running a 5K or 10K race (if already running) to establish a baseline.

What is my goal time for the marathon?

Fitness or just finish: Having no time attached to your goal is not a deterrent from training for a marathon; however, picking a specific time goal or range will help you dial your training in and keep you motivated.

I have a goal time in mind: Make sure you can train the amount needed to reach that goal. This includes ancillaries such as sleep, strength work, and flexibility training.

How much time can I dedicate to training?

<60 minutes on any given day: This puts you in a compromised position. Consider having a longer training segment to build fitness and maximize your training.

>60 min/day. More on weekends: Great! We'll build you up to the appropriate mileage and training gradually. We'll also be able to ultimately make your training segment shorter.

Am I prone to injury?

YES: Investigate the root cause of the injury or injuries. You may need to sacrifice some running at first to emphasize strength and flexibility.

NO: Be sure to maintain a balance of running and strength/flexibility to be able to handle the demands of marathon training.

on crosstraining in Chapter 11)—but it is vital to get advice from an expert if you hope to reach your marathon goal. If you have suffered training injuries in the past, take care not to jump to conclusions about the culprit. The injuries may not be the running itself, but rather improper footwear, poor training practices, or other issues. Consult your doctor and get to the root of the problem so that you don't keep falling into the same injurious trap.

After considering the ins and outs of training, injuries, and motivation mentioned here, one important fact should be clear: At no point did we suggest that certain people aren't good candidates for running a marathon. Even if you're starting from scratch, there is a way for you to successfully complete the 26.2-mile distance. The only instances in which we would advise against starting to do some sort of training are if you're injured, sick, unmotivated to put in the time and effort, or a combination of these factors. You can work around hurdles such as lack of experience or past injuries if you're currently healthy and motivated. All it takes is the right plan adjusted to your particular needs to put you on a successful journey toward the marathon.

Putting Everything into Perspective

Taking time to assess your readiness to start marathon training allows you to choose a program to meet you where you are. In Chapter 7, you'll find several plans: the C2THON (which starts with a 0–5K prep plan) for brand-new runners, the From Scratch for relative beginners, the Just Finish for runners who want to do just that, the Advanced First Timer for more experienced runners, and the Express for runners coming directly off training for shorter races. To help you pick the best plan, we've compiled some key takeaway points for each of the three types of aspiring marathoners mentioned earlier.

The Beginner

You're going to need time to get ready to start training and there will certainly be unknowns as you wade in. The biggest question marks will concern your goals and how your body will respond to training. Your best and ultimately shortest path to success is seemingly the longest. Again and again we've witnessed runners jump into a new program they aren't ready for and end up injured a month or two later. Allow yourself the time to prepare your body and mind and build accordingly. It'll save you time and suffering in the end, we promise. Here are the initial steps to take.

❱ Step 1: Make running a habit

Your first priority should be to block out eight weeks for an initial training phase that will take you from couch to 5K. This will give you time to progress at a sensible rate, establish good habits, and learn the basic components of fitness running. Look for the C2THON program in Chapter 7, which includes the "0–5K" plan, your 8-week buildup.

❱ Step 2: Establish a starting point for marathon training

Once you've completed those first two months of training, run a 5K race in order to establish a realistic marathon goal. In most places there are 5K events almost every weekend, so finding one shouldn't be a problem. In addition to helping you establish a baseline for training, it's also a great way for you to learn the ropes of racing.

❱ Step 3: Start marathon training!

Once you have run your 5K, you can turn your attention to marathon-specific training.

The Recreational Runner

You are probably already putting in several runs of 30 minutes or more each week, which puts you ahead of the curve. That training provides a great foundation on which to turn yourself into a marathoner.

❱ Step 1: Establish a training goal

Either draw from a race time you recently logged or sign up for a 5K or 10K race to test your current fitness. That time can then be plugged into a race equivalency calculator to help you pinpoint a goal for training. We'll cover specifics on goal setting in Chapter 9.

❱ Step 2: Choose the right plan

That aforementioned race time, your current weekly mileage, and the number of weeks and months you have to train before the big event will determine the best training plan for you. For those running 10–20 miles per week, we suggest using the Just Finish plan, which will meet you at that mileage level and progress you to where you need to be to complete a marathon in 18 weeks.

For those running more than 20 miles per week, we suggest the From Scratch plan or the Advanced First Timer plan, depending on current mileage and where you think your ability is. For many recreational runners, the From Scratch plan will be the best choice.

❱ Step 3: Start training!

You'll continue to learn plenty along the way, but you are ready to start your marathon buildup right now. As you develop greater fitness and confidence, you will transition from a fitness/shorter distance runner to a marathoner.

The Competitive Runner

If you're already a competitive runner, you'll likely find the biggest challenge is navigating the difference in training for a 5K, 10K, or half-marathon and the training for the marathon. Not only are the training and commitment different when it comes to the 26.2-mile event, but you can also expect your body and mind to handle it in new and unexpected ways.

❱ Step 1: Establish your baseline

Most competitive runners have a 5K or 10K race time from the past couple months on which they can base their marathon goals.

❱ Step 2: Find the right schedule

The majority of runners in this group probably log from 30 to 50 miles per week. While that volume might determine your ultimate goal pace, everyone in this group needs about the same number of weeks to prepare for the marathon. Eighteen weeks is a perfect amount of time to prep you for the big race, which is why we suggest the Advanced First Timer plan. If you are down to the last few months, the Express plan might be an option, too.

❱ Step 3: Start training!

With the benefit of experience and mileage on your legs, you're ready to jump right into training.

Keep all of this in mind as you select your training program. Whatever your background, experience and goal, we've got you covered when it comes to getting you to the finish line.

2

WHAT KIND OF RUNNER ARE YOU?

BEFORE YOU STEP UP TO THE MARATHON, it is vital that you step back. Reflecting on your individual physiology, as well as your unique training psychology, can go a long way in setting the stage for success at the 26.2-mile distance. This chapter will help you get a handle on your natural inclinations as a runner. While some folks are endowed with ideal endurance genes— think of the athletes who win the Boston and New York City marathons— most of the rest of us aren't perfect marathon specimens. The good news is that even if you don't have long, lean legs, a perfect stride, or a natural proclivity for mentally focusing over many miles, you can successfully finish a marathon with the right training.

Let's first consider physiology by looking in the mirror. Body type— including frame, shape, and musculature—can determine a lot about how we will respond to endurance training. While increased health and fitness can certainly change our bodies, it's worth taking stock of which of three categories you naturally fall into: mesomorph, endomorph, or ectomorph.

About 15 percent of people are mesomorphs, characterized by wide shoulders, narrow hips, and a muscular build. Mesomorphic athletes tend to be strong and powerful, but have a light frame. Think of a typical sprinter. These runners possess a high volume of fast-twitch muscle fibers, but are also endowed with a high starting VO_2max, which is a measure of how your body utilizes oxygen. The higher your VO_2max, the more efficiently your body delivers oxygen to your working muscles, which contributes to running performance. While mesomorphs will benefit from their high VO_2max during marathon training, the fact that their musculature tends to favor fast-twitch over slow-twitch fibers indicates that they might need to adjust expectations for the marathon when basing goal times on shorter performances.

The endomorph has a wider waist and shoulders, thicker rib cage, and shorter limbs. They tend to have a larger frame and above-average weight. About 70 percent of us fall into this category. Since endomorphs are considered "average" in many respects, they tend to respond to training programs

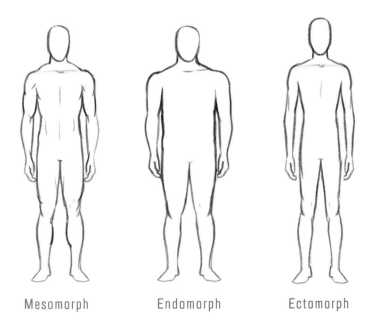

Mesomorph   Endomorph   Ectomorph

in predictable ways because most plans are based on the "average" runner. They can generally expect to successfully progress through training as long as they increase mileage and intensity at sensible rates.

Finally, you have the other 15 percent of the population, which is what would be considered the true "marathon body" type, the ectomorph. Characterized by skinny, long limbs and a light frame, these runners tend to react a little more slowly to training than average (the endomorph), but over time excel in aerobic-dominant events. Physiologically, they have a great volume of slow-twitch muscle fibers and a slightly lower starting VO_2max. Since they tend to recover more quickly than average and handle high volumes of training with ease, the ectomorph usually improves as the distance increases from shorter races to longer ones like a marathon.

Obviously not everyone will fit into a specific mold—maybe you see some of yourself in a couple of the categories—but these types offer useful general descriptions. A quick look in the mirror can "reflect" a lot of data before you even take your first steps in a marathon training program.

Once you've made a physical assessment of your own physiology, it's important to consider the ways in which you might respond to training. Understanding how your body and mind respond to physical exertion can help you not only set appropriate goals, but also assist in tweaking training to optimize your unique potential. This short quiz will help you pinpoint strengths and weaknesses as you enter into marathon training. If you're new to running and aren't sure how to answer these, just keep them in the back of your mind as you begin to train. You can also reflect on other sports or exercise programs you've participated in to give you some data to work with. Ultimately, your strengths and weaknesses will reveal themselves as you begin to log some miles.

For each question, circle the number next to your answer.

? What type of training do you prefer?

1. Long tempo runs and intervals
2. Short and fast repeats

It's only natural to enjoy things that you are good at. For instance, if you are a runner who tends to prefer longer workouts, it's likely because you have a greater volume of slow-twitch muscle fibers and therefore tend to perform better as the distance gets longer. Or, if you aren't currently running, maybe you noticed that you prefer long, leisurely bike rides to all-out 30-minute spin classes. On the other hand, if you're an athlete who has more fast-twitch fibers, then you are probably naturally inclined to prefer short and speedy workouts, whether that's running sprints on the track or riding hard in a spin class. If you find yourself in the latter camp, not to worry. While you may struggle with the endurance-based training a bit more early on, with time and training, you can run a great marathon.

? What type of training do you adapt best to?

1. Longer work: tempo runs and long runs
2. Everything in moderate doses
3. Faster work: repeat runs at mile to 5K pace

Answering this can be a bit of a guessing game, but consider the type of workouts you've done (in any sport) in the past and how you felt they affected your fitness level. Some people will feel really fit after just a couple of weeks of long, moderately paced endurance training, while others feel their fitness is boosted by regular high-intensity work. Knowing this gives you some quick insight into your physiological makeup. As you may have guessed, our bodies tend to adapt better to the training we are naturally best at. It doesn't mean that you can't train for a marathon if you tend to best adapt to sprint work, but you may need to commit to a slightly longer training block to ease into the longer training.

? At which distances are you strongest?

1. Far better at longer distances (>10K) than shorter
2. Good across the board, but slightly better at longer distances
3. Good across the board, but slightly better at shorter distances
4. Far better at shorter distances (<10K) than longer

This question further pinpoints where your natural inclination and talent lie and how to best approach training. If you don't have a natural proclivity for running longer distances, be sure to be patient as you build your endurance. It will come with time and training.

? How do you typically approach a race?

1. I tend to hold an even pace throughout or even pick it up in the second half
2. I go out hard and tend to fade toward the end
3. I have a great kick, but struggle to keep up

How you answer this question speaks to your general level of endurance. If you tend to log fairly even race paces, you probably possess a fairly strong aerobic engine. If you chose the second option, also known as the "fly and die" approach, you will probably have to put some effort into building your endurance and aerobic strength. Finally, if you're more of a sprinter, you probably picked the last option, which simply means you'll need to work on your endurance.

? What types of runs do you best recover from?

1. Long runs and marathon-specific workouts
2. Everything about the same
3. Strength and speed workouts

Knowing how you recover from certain workouts will help you plan your training. If you know you need two days of recovery between a long run and a speed workout, plan accordingly. Your recovery time may even dictate the length of certain training segments. For instance, if you recover slowly from marathon-specific training, you may need to lengthen that block of training. Conversely, if you recover quickly from that type of training, you might shorten it. This allows you to maximize your development as a marathoner, and helps you skirt injuries, overtraining, and training plateaus. In Chapter 12, we will discuss how to structure training around workouts that you don't naturally recover from as well.

Scoring

Tally your scores from all questions. Then find where your score falls in the ranges below to determine where your strengths may lie as a runner.

>6: In for the Long Haul

7–10: Jack of All Trades

11–15: Fast and Furious

A lower score indicates a natural propensity for endurance events, while a higher score might mean you're more of a sprinter. But remember, even the highest-scoring runner is not precluded from the marathon. This quiz is purely meant to help you gather information to properly structure training.

Final Thoughts

The goal of asking yourself these probing questions is to help you get a clearer handle on your natural abilities, not only to set expectations, but also to tweak your training in order to maximize what you do well and minimize what is weaker. It is important to be aware of your individual strengths and weaknesses before jumping into training so that you can chart the best path forward. If you're working with a coach, then these are great questions to discuss with him or her. The answers will assist them in guiding your training. If you aren't using a coach, not to worry. We've developed the programs in this book with the express goal of accommodating different types of runners. Throughout, we will explain how you can tweak your training to address various strengths, weaknesses, and other situations.

The
Why

3

OUR TRAINING PHILOSOPHY

THE HANSONS TRAINING PROGRAMS HAVE BEEN providing consistent results for runners of all abilities and experience levels for more than 25 years. While Keith and Kevin knew the plans worked thanks to plenty of anecdotal evidence, I was brought on board in 2006 to help identify the science behind *why* they worked. The biggest lesson I have learned as the programs' exercise science guy, as well as a runner and coach myself, is that the best coaches have already figured out what training is effective, even if they don't know exactly what is happening inside the muscles, heart, bones, and brain. Exercise scientists like me merely come in later to answer physiological questions and back up what coaches are already doing. Hansons is a smart, vetted system that works, and we know why it works, which has shaped the Hansons training philosophy.

To give you a greater understanding of this philosophy, we'll break it down into two components: education and competition. The education piece is the how and why of training and the competition component is all about how to actually get you running at your best.

Education: How and Why to Train

While you may not be particularly interested in the detailed reasoning behind our training system, it's important to have some understanding of why you're doing the training you're doing. Mindlessly logging mileage and workouts without a sense of purpose is a recipe for burnout. Ask yourself questions like "Why am I doing this workout?" and "What purpose does it serve?" and know the answers. When you understand the reasoning behind your training, you'll not only be more likely to adhere to the prescribed workouts, you'll also carry those lessons into future training.

The marathon, executed well, often spawns lifelong runners. Soon after crossing that finish line, you just may find yourself plotting your next race. That's why we want to make sure to do a thorough job of introducing you to the most important foundational principles that underscore training—so that you can apply these to other races and distances down the line. Our central goal is to provide you with a successful first marathon training experience, but at the same time, set you up with the tools to keep running into the future.

Competition: How to Compete

We all define competition in our own ways. For one runner, it might mean competing to win a race; for another, it may be competing for an age-group title. When it comes to the marathon, however, many of us are competing for intangibles such as pride, self-worth, and triumph over challenge. The Hansons programs are designed to train you to be a competitor, regardless of what that might mean to you. You will learn to handle discomfort and fatigue, to overcome challenges, and to push yourself past your perceived limits.

Is the Hansons training system only for fast runners? Absolutely not. Our programs are for any runner who wants to run faster and is willing to fully commit to training. It is a system built for competitors regardless of how you define that. It is for those who understand that those weeks and weeks of training surely won't be all rainbows and unicorns. And for those who know that there will be some blood, sweat, and tears involved, but that they will arrive at the start line fully prepared to compete. We want runners to read this book because they are fired up, ready to go, and excited about traveling down this path of success.

The Method

The concept of cumulative fatigue drives much of the training that makes up the Hansons Marathon Method. As the name suggests, cumulative fatigue is fatigue that develops over long periods of training at moderate paces (as opposed to a more acute physiological fatigue that occurs during a shorter race). Consider running a 5K race at top speed—your lungs are burning and your legs feel like jelly by the end. It is a very pronounced type of discomfort. Then there's the type of fatigue that develops over several hours of running at a slower pace. It's a totally different feeling of exhaustion. While the fatigue that results from running a short race is caused by the buildup of by-products and waste in your muscles, marathon fatigue is caused by the depletion of fuel. When you train your body to withstand cumulative fatigue, you prepare it for the demands of a long race such as a marathon.

Four training support posts make productive cumulative fatigue possible. If you are missing even one of these, the whole system becomes shaky and you risk injury, overtraining, or burnout. The training support posts are:

❯ Training balance

❯ Appropriate intensity

❯ Consistency

❯ Mileage

Training Balance

It seems that the long run gets the most attention when people talk about marathon training. It's the star of the show. So it can be easy to think that what you do during the week doesn't matter all that much as long as you get in that weekend long run. There's the feeling that, "if I can run 20 miles, I can make it to 26.2." The problem with this strategy is that it merely trains you to survive the marathon. We contend that with the right training you can not only survive it, but also thrive at the distance.

In our view, the long run's importance in the larger landscape of training is often overemphasized, while the importance of the rest of the workouts is diminished. The long runs in our programs are capped at 16 miles, which has caused some raised eyebrows and not a little bit of disbelief. But when you dig into our method and look at the training that surrounds the long run, our reasoning for capping long runs at 16 miles becomes clear.

We look at the long run as just one piece of the training puzzle, in addition to elements such as speed, marathon pace runs, and easy days. If we add in these various components of training at the right times, we can then build into the long run. While you might not feel 100 percent fresh for that long run, the fatigue in your legs from those other workouts will mimic how you'll feel during the latter miles of the marathon. That is why for most people following our plans, 16 miles provides adequate time on your feet for the long run. It's not a random number, but rather the sweet spot of enough mileage to contribute to endurance without compromising other important workouts throughout the week. The overall outcome? A more balanced training plan that puts equal weight on a wide variety of workouts. We've seen proof in the results of the runners we coach. The athletes who have embraced these tactics and completed our programs have found that they can do more than they ever thought possible.

Appropriate Intensity

The key to successful training balance in the Hansons method is running the right intensity on the right days. New runners in particular tend to run their easy days too hard because the early days of a progressive training plan can feel relatively relaxed. Even the most experienced runners are known for running too hard in certain workouts and pushing themselves to the point of overtraining. While this book will help you calculate the correct paces to run, it's important to keep in mind that intuition and feel also play roles in determining appropriate intensity.

For instance, you'll notice in the plans that your paces for easier days are prescribed in a range. This means that if you're feeling great on one of those days, you can choose to run on the faster end of the pace range. Conversely, if you're feeling zapped from a previous workout, you might decide to run on the slower end. While easy days are sometimes dubbed "junk mileage," they are a big percentage of training and are therefore quite important. When these runs are completed at the optimal intensity, they promote a wide array of favorable physiological adaptations.

Proper pacing during hard workouts is equally vital. Just because they are supposed to be "hard" doesn't give you license to run yourself into the ground. The paces for an interval workout, for instance, are tailored to produce certain results. If you run the first few repeats way too fast and the last few too slow because you're tired, you haven't run any of them at the prescribed pace and won't reap the desired benefits.

The goal is to increase both mileage and intensity across many weeks and months. Adhering to an easy pace on an easy day is essential as you build strength and endurance in the early days of training. Once you add in hard workouts, these easy days will serve as active recovery to allow your body to bounce back and prepare for the next workout. Similarly, if you hope to rack up the physiological adaptations that will make you the best marathoner you can be, running hard workouts too fast won't serve your cause. These training plans are challenging enough, so don't make them harder than they need to be.

Training at the appropriate intensities will not only offer you great benefits for your physical fitness, it will also teach you self-control, awareness, and patience, and it will train you to become a natural judge of pace. These things will all serve you well on race day.

Consistency

As you might guess, the more days, weeks, and months of solid training that you can string together, the better. But with the many pulls on our time every day, how do you make consistency a reality?

I've had the pleasure of training alongside Olympic marathoners and aside from talent, one thing they had in common was their incredible consistency. When they were at their best, they were able to string together weeks, months, and even years of solid and consistent training. Of course most of us don't have the luxury of devoting the same resources to training that the pros do. As parents, spouses, homeowners, and business owners, we understand that life sometimes intervenes. We don't expect a training plan to be adhered to 100 percent. Rather, it's about finding consistency by making your training a priority and then doing the best you can do amidst the unpredictable nature of everyday life.

Taking a balanced approach to training and running the appropriate intensities in workouts—the first two support pillars—will also make it a lot easier to be consistent in your training. Consistency, the third pillar, isn't just important in your schedule; it's important to your adaptations. Physiologically speaking, inconsistency in training makes for a never-ending struggle to maintain even a baseline of fitness. While adaptations can occur rapidly with proper and consistent training, they can be lost during just a few weeks of inconsistent running. For instance, if a runner trains five days a week for three weeks, a noticeable improvement in fitness will take place. But if those weeks are followed by a couple of weeks of running only two or three days a week, those fitness gains will begin to retreat. It then would require two more weeks of consistent running to get back to the previous level of fitness. In the end, six to eight weeks of running went by just to get you back to where you were at week three.

So how do you harness consistency? Establishing goals that are challenging, yet attainable, is key. This will keep you motivated without discouraging or overwhelming you. Properly placed goals will help you get out the door each day, even on the days when running feels like the last thing you want to do or have time for.

Planning your weekly running schedule in advance will also help with commitment and consistency. Rather than looking at your training schedule the morning of a workout, know what to expect for the next five to seven days. By penciling your runs into your day planner, putting them in your smartphone calendar, or posting them on the refrigerator, you can plan for and possibly avoid hurdles that may be thrown at you throughout the week. If you know you have an early meeting Tuesday morning, plan on running after work that day. If your kids have a soccer tournament all weekend, find an opening between games to fit your run in. And when life does intervene, modify training, but don't skip it unless you absolutely have to. Something is always better than nothing.

Mileage

Adequate mileage, pillar number 4, plays a vital role in the cumulative fatigue process. But what does "adequate" mean? How many miles do you need to run to properly train for a marathon? The general answer is, a moderate to high amount. Consider that runners training for a 5K race run around 4–6 times their actual race distance in mileage each week. People training for a marathon need to increase their mileage beyond the 26.2-mile distance as well. Although the competitive marathoner won't put in 4–6 times the marathon distance on a weekly basis (100–150 miles), it is reasonable to run 2–3 times the distance per week (50–70 miles). (See Table 3.1.)

If you think 50–70 miles per week sounds intimidating, you're not alone. While most runners preparing for the marathon realize they need to

TABLE 3.1 **WEEKLY MILEAGE BASED ON LEVEL AND EVENT**

	Beginner	Competitive	Elite
5K	20–30	40–50	90+
Marathon	40–50	60–70	110+

increase their volume of mileage to be ready to toe the starting line, they lack confidence in their ability to run as much as they are going to need to. If you find yourself in that camp, try embracing this mentality: Start at the ridiculous and work back until you reach something manageable. If right now, 60 miles in a week seems ridiculous, focus on what are you supposed to do today, and today only. You will be surprised at what you can handle a few months down the line.

Keep in mind that your body will be able to handle increased mileage only if you're training smart. Running workouts too fast, training in old shoes, and adding too much mileage too quickly can all derail your buildup. When athletes give their bodies time to adapt to new training stresses, they are able to handle far more than they ever imagined possible. The Hansons programs work to take you up the mileage ladder one rung at a time, gradually increasing both mileage and intensity. As we like to say to our athletes, "If you want to build a house, you must first create a structure to hold it up." The volume of mileage builds a foundation that allows all the other variables to work.

To get you running that good amount of mileage, though, we don't add extra hard workouts, but rather, more easy mileage. The Hansons Marathon Method will show you how to safely add mileage, while still keeping your pace in check to avoid burning yourself out.

Some marathon training programs are tailored to fit what runners want, rather than what they need. To accommodate runners' typical free time, these programs often place roughly half of the weekly mileage on Saturday and Sunday. The other half of the mileage is then spread over a few days of the workweek. Since such plans are trying to fit in all of the high-intensity work-outs into fewer days, the easy days often fall by the wayside. The result of those harder workouts is the need for greater recovery time, so even if they do instruct athletes to take easy running days, it's likely their legs would be too zapped to complete them.

With our programs, if you get the first three support posts right—that is, you're able to balance your training, stick to the right intensities, and run consistently—then mileage will naturally build in an appropriate manner.

Bringing It Back to Cumulative Fatigue

Bringing together the various support elements of cumulative fatigue in training is a fine balancing act. Remove even one of the variables and the whole formula becomes null. The parts are interrelated, so they build upon and rein-force one another. Consistently striking a good balance between easy and hard days and running those days at the appropriate intensities will naturally lead to adequate weekly mileage totals. In most cases, doing these things will also keep you from getting injured or overtrained, thereby keeping you on track in all respects.

Will you be tired? Certainly. The important thing to remember is that "tired" is a wholly different phenomenon than "overtrained." Training for a marathon isn't easy, and it shouldn't be taken lightly. A few curse words may be uttered, favorite television shows missed, and social outings forgone, but you will regret nothing when you successfully cross that finish line. This program is developed by great coaches who have learned from other great coaches and decades of working with athletes. It is a philosophy that can transform you from a person who wants to run a marathon to a bona fide marathoner.

We're going to get you there.

4

PHYSIOLOGY

MOST TRAINING BOOKS WILL INCLUDE a chapter on physiology. But the information isn't always rendered in a way that runners can easily understand and readily employ. Sometimes when I read a journal article or a textbook, I have a hard time seeing the practical application for the average runner. I find myself wondering, "Does doing this or that even make sense for the average person?" I figured if I had these questions, then a lot of other people did too. So I set out to write a chapter on physiology that gives readers "aha" moments. I want you to be able to close the book, take a breath, and say, "This all makes sense now. I know what I need to do and why I need to do it."

It can all get a little confusing. And we (and by *we* I mean coaches, exercise physiologists, lab rats, and brainiac runners) tend to overthink training processes. We oftentimes know too much for our own good. But you don't need a PhD in exercise physiology to train better. This chapter will help you learn the basics of the physiology involved so that you can direct your attention toward the training itself. By grasping the basic physiological justification for each day's run, you will gain confidence in your training, sans information overload.

Now, as both an exercise physiologist and a coach, I know that sometimes there can be disagreement between what the science says and what the real world dictates. With this chapter, my goal is to bridge that gap by not just telling you about science-based principles, but more importantly, helping you connect them to your own real-world performance.

You will find that we tailor our plans specifically to entertain the many physiological adaptations your body needs to make to run a successful 26.2 miles. Keep in mind the following principles as you dive into our methods:

❭ Marathon muscles

❭ VO_2max

❭ Anaerobic threshold

❭ Aerobic threshold

❭ Running economy

Marathon Muscles

When it comes to physiological movers and shakers, the musculature system is king. More than 600 muscles in your body work to create motion and force. They allow your heart to beat, your eyes to move, your food to digest, and your legs to run. The three main types of muscle fibers are cardiac, smooth, and skeletal. While the cardiac muscle makes your heart beat and the smooth muscle lines your intestines, pushing food through your system, the skeletal muscle plays the biggest role in human locomotion. Skeletal muscles make running possible.

Not only are the skeletal muscles responsible for generating physiological movement, but they are also where the majority of energy is stored. These muscles include slow-twitch fibers and fast-twitch fibers, the latter of which has several subcategories. Each muscle contains both types of muscle fiber, which are bound together like bundles of cable, each bundle consisting of a single type. Thousands of these bundles constitute a muscle, and each individual bundle is controlled by a single motor neuron. The motor neurons are located in the central nervous system where they work to control muscles and in turn, movement.

Altogether, the fibers and the motor neuron make up the motor unit. Since each bundle contains only one type of fiber, a bundle of slow-twitch fibers and a bundle of fast-twitch fibers will receive information from the brain via separate motor units. If one motor neuron is activated, a weak muscle contraction occurs. If multiple motor neurons are activated, however, a more powerful muscular contraction is created.

Why is all this important? Ultimately, the structure of the skeletal muscle system dictates marathon ability. The better understanding you have of your own physiology, the smarter your training will be. Let's look more closely at the muscle types.

Type I Fibers (Slow-Twitch Fibers)

Your family tree plays an important role in determining your marathon potential. If your parents endowed you with an abundance of slow-twitch muscle fibers, you have a leg up on the competition. These slow-twitch fibers, also called type I fibers, are particularly important for endurance events because of their efficient use of fuel and their resistance to fatigue. Slow-twitch muscle fibers are aerobic, which means they use oxygen to transfer energy. This is a result of their large capillary area, which provides a much greater available supply of oxygen than fast-twitch fibers. Additionally, these fibers have the machinery necessary for aerobic metabolism to take place. Known as the mitochondria, this machinery is often referred to as the "powerhouse of the cell." Thanks to the mitochondria, you are able to use fats and carbohydrates as fuel sources to keep your body running.

True to their name, the slow-twitch fibers also have a slower shortening speed than the other types of fibers, which serves an important function for endurance runners. While these fibers cannot generate as much force as the others, they supply energy at a steady rate and can generate a good amount of power for an extended period. They also have smaller motor neurons, which require less neural impulse to make them contract, so the slow-twitch fibers are first to start contracting when you begin running. In addition to being slower to contract, type I fibers are only about half the diameter of fast-twitch fibers. Although they are smaller and slower, they are also more efficient and persistent, warding off fatigue during a long haul on the roads.

Type II Fibers (Fast-Twitch Fibers)

Fast-twitch fibers, also known as type II fibers, are also genetically determined and are the slow-twitch fibers' more ostentatious counterpart. They are bigger, faster, and pack a powerful punch, but they also fatigue rapidly. Since these fibers have very few mitochondria, they transfer energy anaerobically, without the use of oxygen. These forceful contractions use such large amounts of adenosine triphosphate (ATP), basically a high-energy molecule, that they quickly tire and become weak. That is precisely why an Olympic 100-meter champion can run a record-setting pace for the length of the homestretch, while a marathon champion can maintain a record-setting pace for 26.2 miles. Two different muscle-fiber types; two different results.

The type II fibers are further divided into subgroups. Two of the most common are type IIa and type IIb, also known as the intermediate fibers. The type IIa fibers share several characteristics with slow-twitch fibers, as they have more mitochondria and capillaries than other types of fast-twitch fibers. As a result, type IIa fibers are considered to be aerobic, although they still

TABLE 4.1 **COMPARISON OF MUSCLE FIBER TYPES**

	Type I	Type IIa	Type IIb
Contraction time	Slow	Fast	Fastest
Fatigue resistance	High	Medium	Low
Force production	Low	High	Highest
Mitochondria density	High	High	Low
Capillary density	High	Medium	Low
Oxidative capacity	High	High	Low

provide a more forceful contraction than slow-twitch fibers. By contrast, type IIb fibers contract powerfully, transfer energy anaerobically, and fatigue quickly. See Table 4.1 for a brief comparison of fiber types.

A working system

All humans have both type I and type II muscle fibers, but the distribution varies greatly. Most people, regardless of gender, have a type I fiber distribution of 45–55 percent in their arms and legs. Individuals who are fitness conscious, but not completely devoted to training, can see a type I distribution of around 60 percent. Meanwhile, trained distance runners tend to have a type I distribution of 70 percent, and elite marathoners have an even greater percentage than that. Herein lies the challenge. When it comes to running a marathon, Runner A, who has a high proportion of type I fibers, will naturally be better off than Runner B, who has a low type I and low type IIa distribution. So how does Runner B get around his own physiology?

Luckily for both runners, the body is an amazing machine capable of adapting to a myriad of stresses. In the field of exercise physiology, "stress" denotes the repeated and intense training that leads to certain physiological adaptations. Researchers have long sought the key to muscle-fiber conversion, hoping they might discover how a person like Runner B could actually change the composition of his or her muscles via training stress. Although much of the research remains inconclusive, it is agreed that elite distance runners have a greater proportion of type I fibers than the average recreational runner, and that those type I fibers are necessary for a fast marathon performance. (See Table 4.2 for a comparison among different types of runners.) What we don't know is if you are genetically bound to a particular muscle-fiber arrangement or if you can change it with physical training through certain training stresses. Although it may be too early to make any definite statements about conversions from type I to type II fibers, it has been shown that transformations can take place within type II fibers. Even after a relatively short training block of 10–12 weeks, a runner can display a transition from anaerobic, fatigable type IIb fibers to the more aerobic, fatigue-resistant type IIa fibers. This is great for an endurance runner. It shows that training elicits tangible physiological changes that create performance advantages and real improvements. There is much hope for Runner B.

Maximizing muscle fibers

Regardless of genetics, training remains a vital predictor of running performance. To get your muscles to respond the way you want them to on race day, you must train them to fire in a particular manner. It all starts with a signal sent from the motor units in the central nervous system, which begins by recruiting the slow-twitch fibers. You continue to rely heavily on those fibers unless one of these three things happens:

1. You increase your pace

2. You encounter a hill or other force that creates resistance

3. You run long enough to exhaust the slow-twitch fibers

TABLE 4.2 **MUSCLE FIBER COMPOSITION BY TYPE OF ATHLETE**

	Type I	Type IIa	Type IIb
Sprinter	20%	45%	35%
Sedentary	40%	30%	30%
Average active	50%	40%	10%
Middle-distance runner	60%	35%	5%
World-class marathoner	80%	20%	<1%

Depending on fitness level, some runners can go an hour at a modest pace before they begin to recruit the fast-twitch fibers; others can go up to two. It is likely that you'll rely on type I fibers almost exclusively during the first half or so of the marathon. As those fibers tire, the body will begin to employ the type IIa fibers, those slightly larger, aerobic fast-twitch fibers. If you have trained properly, you'll have enough leeway to get through the rest of the marathon using these fibers. While they aren't great for endurance running, they are a good substitute for the exhausted type I fibers. Issues arise when the under-trained runner is forced to go to the third line of defense: type IIb fibers. Remember, these are built for power, and they fatigue quickly. If you are relying on these fibers to get you to the finish line, things will not end well.

What our method seeks to do is teach you how to maximize the use of the type I and type IIa muscle fibers, without having to resort to the type IIb fibers. While genetics dictate what kind of work you may be innately suited for, the right training helps you maximize your individual potential. We will show you how this can be done, no matter what your DNA might say.

Marathon muscles

VO$_2$Max

If muscle fibers are in the driver's seat when it comes to marathon endurance potential, VO$_2$max works in the pit, constantly providing assistance. VO$_2$max stands for "volume of oxygen uptake," defined as the body's maximum capacity to transport and utilize oxygen while running. When a person's VO$_2$max is described as 50 ml/kg/min, you would read "50 milliliters of oxygen per kilogram of bodyweight per minute." Basically, the higher the number, the better. (See sidebar, "Should I Get My VO$_2$max Tested?") Although VO$_2$max is often considered the gold standard of fitness, it should be noted that it doesn't always serve as the best predictor of marathon performance. In fact, elite marathon runners tend to have a slightly lower VO$_2$max than elite 5K and 10K runners. But although it isn't the single most important predictor of marathon potential, it remains a significant piece of the puzzle.

Since blood carries oxygen to the muscles, one must look at the heart when considering VO$_2$max. Just like the skeletal muscles, the heart muscle can be strengthened with work, thus allowing it to pump more blood and push more oxygen to the muscles. The heart adapts to training stress in the same way the muscles in your legs do. There are a number of positive adaptations related to the heart that occur because of endurance training. Four of these adaptations, shown in Figure 4.1 and described below, are considered the central components of VO$_2$max.

Circulation of the coronary arteries improves. Since these are the arteries that supply the heart, improved circulation means more blood reaches it.

Ventricle walls thicken, particularly the left ventricle. This is the area of the heart that pushes blood out to be circulated around the body. As the ventricle walls thicken, the force of the contractions becomes greater, pumping more blood into the circulating arteries.

The ventricle chamber enlarges. This allows for more oxygenated blood to be stored within the ventricle, which is then circulated throughout the body.

Pulse rate decreases. When the cardiac muscle is strengthened, it doesn't have to work as hard to do its job.

In sum, more blood is pumped with greater force and less effort. Since the heart has bigger chambers that hold more blood, heart rate slows across all running paces, making the entire system more efficient and healthier.

FIGURE 4.1 **VO$_2$MAX COMPONENTS**

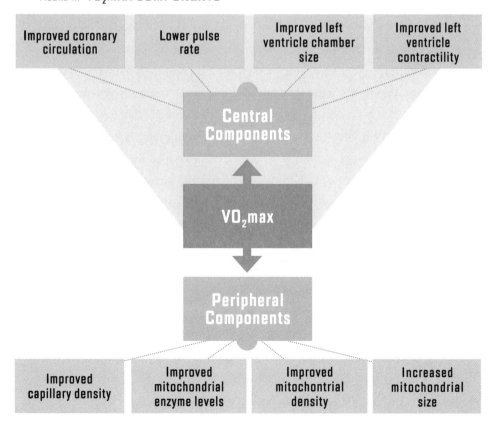

The heart supplies blood to the body, and the better it can deliver large amounts of blood to the bloodstream, the more efficiently the oxygen in the blood reaches the running muscles. What's more, the adaptations don't stop with the heart; they also affect the blood itself. In fact, blood volume has been shown to increase with endurance training. Red blood cells, the most common type of blood cells, are the main means through which oxygen is delivered within the human body. With endurance training, the hematocrit level (the amount of red blood cells within the total volume of blood) decreases. This means that since total blood volume is higher and the blood itself is less viscous, it can travel through the heart and arteries much more easily. Think of the new oil in your car compared with that gunk that's been sitting in the engine for the last 15,000 miles. A lower hematocrit level equates to less wear and tear on your system because, as the red blood cells become larger with training, you lose less oxygen-carrying capacity. While it may sound counterproductive, since plasma volume increases, the hematocrit level decreases because it is expressed as a percentage of volume. So even though the percentage is lower, the total number of red blood cells can be larger. Remember, 20 percent of 100 equals 20 red blood cells and 15 percent of 500 equals 75 red blood cells, giving you more bang for your buck.

With endurance training, the heart becomes a stronger pump and the blood supply becomes bigger and better, but none of that matters if the muscles cannot use the massive amount of oxygen that is now being dropped off at their doorstep. The actual delivery of oxygen to the muscle happens in the capillary bed, which is the end of the line for the artery. Some of these capillaries are so small that only one red blood cell can drop off its bounty of oxygen to the muscle at a time. From there, the red blood cell begins its journey back to the heart and lungs where it is reloaded with oxygen. During rest, many of these capillary lines lie dormant. As you begin running, the lines open up, allowing muscles to accept an increasing amount of oxygen to meet the demands of exercise.

While improving the central components of VO$_2$max is important, having a bigger left ventricle to pump more blood doesn't do much good if the muscles that are being used can't handle the changes. Luckily, our running muscles, as we discussed, adapt simultaneously. These adaptations, shown in Figure 4.1 and which we will call peripheral components, include

Increased capillary density: A greater density of capillaries means that oxygen can move among cells faster and more efficiently. This allows the exercising muscle to receive the oxygen it needs to continue to exercise.

Improved mitochondrial enzyme levels and activity: Think of an enzyme as a tool that makes work easier, rather like the ramp you'd use to push a heavy box up the front steps. Enzymes reduce the amount of energy required to make a reaction occur. With higher levels, reactions within the mitochondria can allow more work to be done at the same rate.

Improved mitochondrial density: The mitochondria are where fats and carbohydrates are presented as fuel for exercise, so the more mitochondria we have, the more fat can be used as fuel to maintain aerobic intensity.

Increased size of existing mitochondria: Bigger mitochondria allow more fuel to be processed at a single site. If we can process more fatty acids through more and bigger mitochondria, we reduce the need for carbohydrates to be used and increase the intensity it takes to prompt the anaerobic system (which relies on carbohydrates for energy).

The bottom line is that the body is remarkable at adapting to training. It will do everything it can to support a given activity and become better at it. VO$_2$max is the ceiling for your aerobic potential, but it is not the overall determinant of potential performance. When your aerobic capacities are maxed out, your anaerobic faculties are right on their heels. As a result, other physiological variables contribute to how well a person can run a marathon.

Anaerobic Threshold

Marathon running relies heavily on the oxygen supplied by the aerobic system, which is more efficient and provides greater endurance than the anaerobic system. While powerful and explosive, the anaerobic system functions without oxygen and therefore can provide only short bursts of speed before energy stores are depleted, lactic acid builds up in the muscles, and running ceases. Although lactic acid, or lactate, has gotten a bad rap as a soreness-inducing, fatigue-causing by-product of high-intensity exercise, it actually serves as an energy source for the muscles, allowing them to squeak out a bit more work before bonking. Research now tells us that the fatigue that occurs at that point is caused by another physiological phenomenon. The real culprits are the electrolytes: sodium, potassium, and calcium. These electrolytes are positioned along the muscles, each with its own electrical charge that triggers muscle contractions. At high intensities and over time, the potassium ion outside the cell builds up, clogs the passageway, and cannot switch places with the sodium ion inside the cell. This leads to weaker and weaker muscle contractions, or neuromuscular fatigue, and it will soon slow your body to a sputtering halt. Not only is blood lactate not the villain we once thought it to be, we've also come to realize that it plays an important role in marathon running. The aerobic system supports a moderate pace for long periods because the lactate that is produced is simultaneously processed and removed. However, as the aerobic system fatigues or the intensity increases, you become more dependent on the anaerobic system, and in turn reach a point where you produce lactate faster than your body is able to get rid of it. Referred to as lactate threshold, onset of blood lactate, or anaerobic threshold (AT), it is the tipping point where lactic acid starts to build up in your bloodstream.

Anaerobic threshold is particularly important because it has been identified as perhaps the best predictor of endurance performance. It occurs at anywhere between 60 and 90-plus percent of a person's VO_2max, so as you get closer to your VO_2max, blood lactate begins to accumulate. The best of the best tend to have an anaerobic threshold exceeding 70 percent of VO_2max. While training may raise your VO_2max only a few points, it can have a significant impact on anaerobic threshold. A group of elite marathon runners may have similar VO_2max levels. What tends to separate first place from tenth place is anaerobic threshold. While VO_2max may separate the national class from recreational runners, anaerobic threshold separates the champions from the contenders.

Remember that anaerobic threshold is the point at which the aerobic pathways are still providing energy for muscle contraction, but they cannot do it fast enough to provide all the required energy. This is where the anaerobic pathways begin to make up the difference. As a result, we can push the threshold higher via training. By running farther and faster, we teach our bodies to rely more heavily on the aerobic pathways, thus improving endurance and increasing the time it takes to reach that point of anaerobic reliance. One of the big differences in our marathon training, compared with traditional training programs, is that we teach you to stimulate aerobic metabolism through a large volume of aerobic training, not high-end anaerobic work.

Aerobic Threshold

All this talk about energy systems may have you wondering where that energy comes from in the first place. The short answer: fats and carbohydrates. As a marathon runner, you should focus on training the body to use fat as the primary source of energy. Why? Because fat is high in energy, providing nearly twice as many calories per gram as carbohydrates. And while our bodies store very small amounts of carbohydrates for quick energy, the fat stores are nearly endless. Even if you have a small percentage of body fat, your system has plenty

FIGURE 4.2 **FAT AND CARB USE BASED ON INTENSITY**

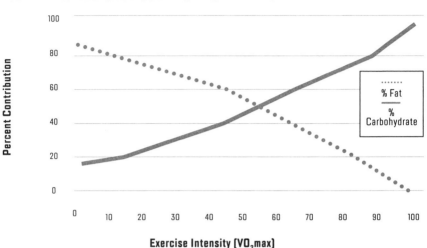

The harder we run, the more we rely on the contribution of carbohydrates. As we approach 100 percent of our maximal aerobic capacity, carbohydrates become the sole source of energy, making carbohydrates the limiting factor in exercise duration and intensity.

of fat for fuel. The only problem is that the oxidation of fat to energy is slow compared with the oxidation of carbohydrates. For most people, fat serves as the main source of energy up to about 50 percent of VO_2max because the fat can be processed fast enough through the mitochondria to supply the demands that running requires up to that point. For most runners, 50 percent of VO_2max is painfully slow. After that point, the body looks to burn carbohydrates. Since fat cannot be burned without oxygen, that point at which the body begins to burn through carb stores is called the aerobic threshold. Figure 4.2 illustrates the contribution of fat and carbohydrate based on running intensity.

This is the reason carbohydrates (glycogen) provide the majority of energy at faster paces. The downside of relying on glycogen stores for energy is that you have only about two hours' worth and once they are gone, your run is over. When you burn through your stored glycogen, the body will draw on the glucose in your blood, which runs out even more quickly. The result is often called "hitting the wall" or "bonking." If you've ever watched a marathon, you have likely seen runners at the front of the pack, the back of the pack, and everywhere in between who smacked right into that wall. They're the ones who have slowed to a slog and look as if they are dragging a 300-pound anchor behind them. Although this was once thought to be an unavoidable rite of passage, a smart training plan will help you skirt the wall altogether. It's all about burning fat for a longer period of time to put off drawing on those limited carbohydrate stores.

Somewhere within the fat-burning range is your optimal marathon pace. If you're a beginning runner, your range may be between 50 and 60 percent of your VO_2max. Trained recreational runners usually range between 55 and 65 percent, and faster runners range between 60 and 80 percent.

Luckily for the aspiring marathoner, it is possible to train the body to burn fat longer. The speed at which fat can be processed doesn't change with training, so in order to be able to use more fat, we have to burn a higher volume of it. To burn a high volume, we need more metabolic factories (the mitochondria, which as mentioned earlier, are "the powerhouse of the cell"). Aerobic training, such as running, helps to add mitochondria, which in turn introduces new enzyme activity and oxygen to the system. While the mitochondria are not necessarily producing energy more quickly, they are bigger and more plentiful, which allows fat to be oxidized and turned into energy for muscle contraction. With the increase in energy from fat, the glycogen in the muscles isn't tapped until later, saving it for faster paces. Basically, the wall is pushed back, and with any luck, never reached.

Figure 4.3 represents the results of a VO_2max treadmill test of a trained recreational runner. Note a linear increase in the amount of oxygen used as intensity increases. At our threshold points, we see slight deflections on the graph. The first represents the aerobic threshold. The second represents the anaerobic threshold. Figure 4.4 represents the blood lactate measurements. By graphing the amount of lactate in the blood at set intervals of a test, we can see the deflection points that coincide with our threshold points.

Running Economy

Running economy, which describes how much oxygen is required to run a certain pace, is the final physiological topic marathoners should understand. Consider this scenario: Runner A and Runner B both have the same VO_2max of 70 ml/kg/min. It might take Runner A 55 ml/kg/min to run a 6:30 mile, while it takes Runner B 60 ml/kg/min to run the same pace. Runner A is more economical than Runner B and probably faster too. See Figure 4.5 for a graphic example.

Although there has been much debate over the effects of running economy, two facts are clear. First, running economy depends on a high training volume. You don't need to pound out 140-mile weeks, but your mileage should be sufficient for the distance you are training. You must also consider the amount of training over weeks, months, and years. Beginners will be less economical than veteran runners, in the same way that a person following a low-mileage plan will be less economical than a person running most days of the week.

FIGURE 4.3 **VO_2MAX RESULTS FROM TREADMILL TEST**

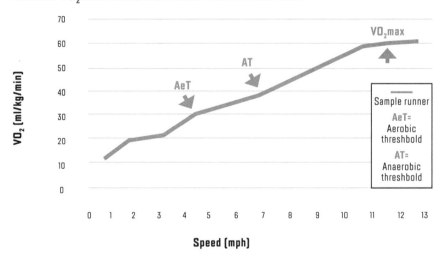

This figure shows a typical treadmill test result for a trained endurance runner. As speed increases, the amount of oxygen consumed increases until a maximal rate, where it then levels off.

FIGURE 4.4 **LACTATE PRODUCTION AND CLEARANCE**

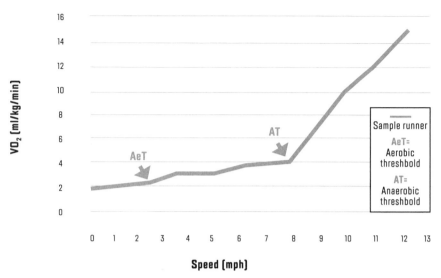

A blood lactate test shows more clearly the deflection points at the same intensities as the VO_2max test. At about 4 mph, there is the first increase in blood lactate, indicating the increased reliance on carbohydrates. At 8 mph, there is the second, more exponential increase, indicating the inability for lactate clearance to match lactate production.

The second component of running economy is speed training. By training at a certain pace, you become more economical at that pace. Since the goal is to improve running economy at race pace, you must spend an adequate amount of time training at race pace. This is why it's important for runners not to run workouts faster than prescribed. When you opt to run faster than suggested, you are training at a level that you may not be ready for, based on actual race performances. Training above suggested paces turns workouts into something they were not intended to be. Easy runs may now resemble tempo runs, tempo runs become strength runs, and strength runs become speed runs. These paces may feel achievable at first, but it is our experience that the majority of people who train too fast end up overtrained, burned out, or injured. If you feel strongly about training at a faster pace, then it is important to run (or simulate) a race to confirm that you are ready to move to a more aggressive pace goal.

FIGURE 4.5 **COMPARISON OF VO$_2$MAX FOR SIMILAR RUNNERS**

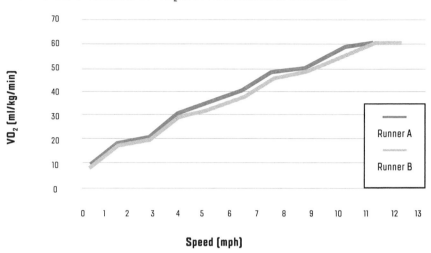

The difference between beating your rivals or losing to them can be a matter of running economy. Here Runner A and Runner B have similar VO$_2$max numbers, but Runner B uses slightly less oxygen at any given speed. This means Runner A is working a little bit harder than Runner B and this may be the difference in winning or losing.

A Physiologically Based Method

If you understand all of the physiological factors involved in optimal marathon training, you can see the underlying reason for each workout. As muscle fibers adapt to running stress, VO$_2$max is optimized, anaerobic threshold improved, and the ability to burn fat at higher intensities is increased. In the end, improved running economy is the result of consistent, optimal training. It all comes down to the tiny, biological happenings of the human body: increased capillarization, an increase in the number and size of mitochondria, and greater mitochondrial enzyme activity equate to less oxygen being necessary to run the same paces. All of these factors play out in our training plans as you run your way to your best 26.2.

SHOULD I GET MY VO$_2$MAX TESTED?

While you may hear a lot about VO$_2$max testing in the worlds of exercise physiology and elite endurance sports, is it something a first-time marathoner needs to worry about? The answer is, "it depends." VO$_2$max is basically the amount of oxygen that your body can use throughout increasingly harder exercise. Along with VO$_2$max testing, most of the time you will also get your aerobic and anaerobic thresholds, as well as your corresponding heart rates, from the test. When I tested athletes, I would also set it up so we could see how fast they were running at different points. This testing can give you some cool data, but how useful is it? After training, your numbers will all improve—that's pretty much a guarantee. You don't need a test to tell you that. The benefit would really come only from conducting multiple tests over a period of time to compare your values against your own previous values. There are also some logistical downsides to spending a lot of time on this type of testing. For instance, the test requires you to wear a mask while breathing through a tube, while trying to run your absolute hardest effort and not fly off the back of the treadmill. Could you run your best under those conditions? It's tough and involves a learning curve. What's more, the test is typically done in controlled environments—indoors and on a treadmill. So those numbers may not equate to the same intensities when training in the real world.

Overall, I would describe the testing as one tool in your tool belt, or better, a method of creating a starting point or checkpoint. If you decide on testing, I suggest getting the Respiratory Exchange Ratio (RER) collected as well. This data will help you determine what percentage of your calories are coming from fat and from carbohydrate, and how many calories you expend at a given intensity level. This information allows you to dial in your fueling, break it down to manageable parts, and even determine if your goal pace is too aggressive. Getting numbers and data is fun, but at the end of the day, you have a fairly good idea of your fitness without it.

The
Programs

5

READY, SET . . .

IN WRITING OUR TRAINING PLANS FOR THIS BOOK, we made a few assumptions about our audience. The first is that you're a first-time marathoner. Another is that you are starting your marathon training fresh and fully recovered. By this we mean that you aren't heading into Day 1 of training immediately after training for and running, say, the spring racing circuit for your local run club. If this is the case, it's wise to take 5–10 days off, with no hard running, before launching into your marathon training.

That said, there's always an exception to the rule. For the slice of readers who are actively training in shorter distances and want to jump into a marathon plan, we have designed the Express Plan. It builds on that shorter distance training and then segues into marathon-specific work. We typically advise these runners to take a 25–35 percent reduction in training volume for a week before starting the Express Plan.

A third assumption we are making when you start one of our programs is that you are healthy. Don't let eagerness get in the way of common sense.

If you have a calf issue that isn't resolved or a quad pull that just won't go away completely, now is not a wise time to launch into marathon training. If you do start your training with an issue, chances are you won't get too many weeks in before having to stop. So if you are even slightly injured, heal up before Day 1 of training. What's more, be sure that you've identified and addressed the root cause of the problem, not just treated the symptoms. Simply taking time off may not be enough.

Common Early Pitfalls

Starting off your training rested and healthy is one of the most important things you can do to ensure your success. However, after decades of coaching, we have noticed that there are several things that runners do early on in a training program that seem harmless at the time, but catch up to them when the training hits the race-specific phase (a.k.a. the hard part). By clueing you into these things, we hope you will avoid making some of the mistakes many runners before you have made.

The first error runners make is taking a Frankenstein approach to training. By that I mean that they haphazardly piece together a training plan, taking what they want from this or that program and leaving aside the rest. For example, some people love the idea of the Hansons 16-mile long run, but aren't as enthused about the 10-mile tempo run. So they may take pieces from another program and use it to replace the tempo run. The problem is, the 16-mile long run works *because* of the 10-mile tempo run, not despite the 10-mile tempo run. This cobbled-together approach leads to a breakdown in the entire training structure. It will serve you much better to stick with our program and trust in the process rather than experimenting along the way with different plans and differing philosophies.

Another trap to steer clear of is getting overzealous in the early days of training. If, as we've advised, you start fresh and fully recovered, then you may be a little antsy once you finally get running. Since we prescribe an early phase of building mileage before we add more intensity, there is a tendency to want to run harder than you should. The result is cumulative fatigue setting in sooner than you want, which can mean you spend too much time in that state. This may cause you to drift over the line into the realm of overtraining. This isn't a point of no return, but if you find yourself overtrained, it will take a significant amount of time to bounce back and return to regular training. We urge you to rein it in, and take it easy those first few weeks of training. There will be plenty of time to run hard later on, you can be sure. A lot of marathon success comes from learning patience, so this is a great early lesson in being patient with training.

A third pitfall also involves taming overzealousness. Once your long, speed, strength, and tempo workouts begin (called "Something of Substance" [SOS] workouts), the tendency is to think that if fast is good, then faster is better. This is simply not the case. We have a name for this: "cheating paces down." If I prescribe 10K pace, a person might go 5K pace. If I say marathon pace, then a person might think that 15-seconds-per-mile faster than that pace is better. While being competitive is good, there's a time and a place for it. I tell my athletes that the initial paces for workouts are going to be faster than ideal because the goal is new. As time goes on, though, they will even out because fitness improves. At the same time, training volume will also be increasing, so it's important not to push the pace even if it feels easier than it once did.

A last potential pitfall is failing to respect how weather conditions influence training. If you are gunning for a late-spring or fall marathon, which many runners aim for, this means that you will begin your training in the dead of winter or summer. As a result, it is likely in either case that your actual race will be run in more ideal weather conditions than much of your training will be. For example, let's say you have your sights set on a fall marathon and your goal marathon pace is 9 minutes per mile. You attempt a tempo run on a hot summer evening, but push an 8:50 pace for the workout. Since in most areas a fall race will be 30+ degrees cooler, that effort might be equivalent to 20–30 seconds faster than goal marathon effort. Early on, you are going to be less acclimated and your fitness won't be as high, so if you push the envelope on paces, it will take its toll. Early on, if you are dealing with challenging weather conditions, give yourself a break. Don't worry if you feel like you are putting in a good effort yet are still a little slow. It's too early to hit the panic button.

While it may be easy to understand these common pitfalls on an intellectual level, avoiding them in practice can be quite difficult. To help you internalize the importance of a smart approach to training, immediately start doing the following three things.

> **Recognize that building fitness is a process.** Be open to the big picture rather than solely focusing on a single day of training.

> **Bad days happen; don't beat yourself up over them.** Pick yourself up the next day and try again. And remember, we learn more from the things we screw up than the things we get right the first time.

> **Allow the schedule to be easy early.** Every day is a step toward a higher level of fitness. Build the foundation first.

When people fall into these common pitfalls, they can easily end up in a prolonged state of cumulative fatigue. Ideally, you will be in that zone only the last 6–8 weeks of training when intensity isn't as high, but your volume and race-specificity training is peaked out. Runners struggle when they are in this state of constant fatigue for 10, 12, or even 14 weeks. That's just too long, and it means that cumulative fatigue will give way to illness, injury, or plain old overtraining, all of which you'll avoid by sticking with the plan and listening to your body.

PACE CHECK

If you tend to be a speed demon or pace cheater, try putting your workouts in your GPS and set a pace range. If it's an easy day, enter your predetermined pace range. For speed and strength days, maybe give yourself a few seconds fast or slow. Tempo runs may allow for 10 seconds per mile fast or slow. (Note: These workouts will be explained in detail in Chapter 6.) By giving yourself a small range, you grant yourself some leeway without getting too far off track. In most cases your watch will vibrate or beep when you drift out of your pace range. This will keep you in check if you know that your lead foot can't be self-governed. If you find you are continually missing your pace ranges for a few weeks in a row, then it may indicate that you need to back off your goal a little bit. This is a good opportunity to learn how to use technology as a tool and not just a crutch. Over time, you'll begin to internalize what those paces feel like and that beeping will become less and less frequent.

6

THE COMPONENTS

THERE IS A COMMON MISCONCEPTION that one can prepare sufficiently for a marathon by simply running three days per week, provided one of those days includes a grueling 20-mile (or more) long run. The simplicity of such a plan may sound appealing, but the truth is that there's a lot more to successful preparation than that. All runs are not created equal, and the long run—while key—is merely one component of a larger system that prepares you for success in the marathon distance.

The plans in this book, while each designed for a different level of runner, are significant training programs. And the Hansons training principles hold true across the board, including our contention that emphasizing one component of training over others, like the long run, won't typically lead to a successful marathon finish.

In this chapter, we will dissect our training schedules, taking a close look at the various components that make up the From Scratch, Just Finish, Advanced First Timer, and Express programs. As you will see, runs are organized in one of two categories: Easy Days and Something of Substance (SOS) workouts. The SOS workouts include long, speed, strength, and tempo runs. (See Figure 6.1 for a breakdown of weekly mileage by workout.) By varying the training plan from one day to the next, you train different bodily systems, all which work in concert to optimize your marathon potential.

The basis for this approach stems from the overload principle, which states that when the body engages in an activity that disrupts its present state of homeostasis (inner balance), certain recovery mechanisms are initiated. Different stressors work to overload the system, stimulating physiological changes. These adaptations, in turn, better prepare the body for that particular stress the next time it is encountered. This is where the principle of cumulative

FIGURE 6.1 **WEEKLY MILEAGE BREAKDOWN**

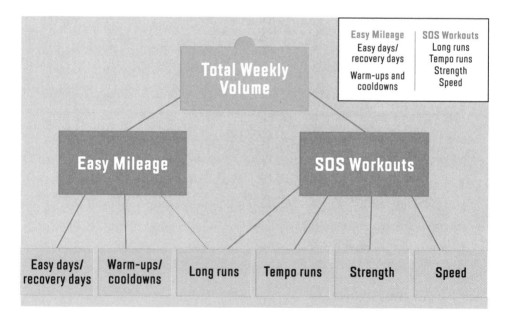

This chart shows the breakdown of weekly mileage. Long runs are under SOS, because by definition they require more effort than a regular easy day. However, they are run at submarathon pace and could be defined as easy.

fatigue, which underscores our entire training philosophy, comes in. Cumulative fatigue is all about challenging the body without reaching the point of no return (overtraining).

Easy Running

Misconceptions abound when it comes to easy running. Such training is often thought of as unnecessary filler mileage. You might even think that easy days can be considered optional, as they don't provide any real benefits. Don't be fooled: Easy mileage plays a vital role in any runner's development. That's good news because it means that not every run needs to be a knock-down, drag-out experience. Easy runs dole out plenty of important advantages without any of the pain by providing a gentler overload that can be applied in a higher volume than SOS workouts. This keeps the body in a constant state of slight disruption, helping to prevent injuries while simultaneously forcing your body to adapt to stress to increase fitness.

Easy running is the base that all training builds upon. After all, a building can be only as big as the foundation it sits on. Especially in a first marathon, that foundation is of the utmost importance. The slow running that you are doing now is what allows you to do the faster workouts later.

The Physiology of Easy Running

When considering why easy running is important, look at what it does for your muscle fibers. As was discussed in Chapter 4, while the number of slow-twitch fibers you are genetically endowed with will ultimately define your potential as a marathoner, training can make a difference. Easy running recruits a host of slow-twitch fibers because they have a lower "firing," or contraction, threshold than the more powerful fast-twitch fibers. Like any other muscle, the more they are used, the more they develop. Along with resistance to fatigue, slow-twitch muscles can be relied upon for more miles

WHY CAN'T I JUST CROSSTRAIN?

If training is all about building aerobic fitness, then can't you accomplish the same thing on an elliptical (or whatever non-running equipment you choose to use)? The short answer is yes, you can. In fact, in our coaching, we often use crosstraining as a way to bridge a runner who isn't running 3–5 times a week to someone who is. However, the longer answer is that crosstraining won't do the job completely. Easy running serves as a way to help a runner build stronger bones and tendons in a way that crosstraining won't do as effectively. For most people, a minimum of 5 days per week of running for the marathon is necessary.

so that the fast-twitch muscles are not fully engaged until down the road. In the end, easy running helps to develop both slow-twitch fibers that are more fatigue resistant and fast-twitch fibers that take on many of the characteristics of the slow-twitch fibers.

Plus, the more slow-twitch fibers you have, the better you'll be prepared to use fat for energy. This is a very good thing because the body contains copious amounts of fat to burn and only a limited supply of carbohydrates. The longer you burn fat rather than carbohydrate, the longer you put off glycogen (carb) depletion and an encounter with the dreaded wall. When you run at lower intensities, you burn somewhere around 70 percent fat and 30 percent carbohydrate. With an increase in pace comes an increase in the percentage of carbohydrates you burn. Your easy running days serve as catalysts to develop those slow-twitch muscle fibers and consequently, teach your body to burn fat instead of carbohydrates. Slow-twitch fibers are better at burning fat than fast-twitch fibers because they contain larger amounts of mitochondria, enzymes that burn fat, and capillaries.

In response to the need for fat to provide the lion's share of the fuel for training, the mitochondria grow larger and are dispersed throughout the muscles. In fact, research has indicated that just six to seven months of training can spur the mitochondria to grow in size by as much as 35 percent and in number by 5 percent. This benefits you as a runner because the higher density of mitochondria works to break down fat more effectively. For instance, if you burned 60 percent fat at a certain pace a year ago, training may have increased that percentage to 70 percent. This is one of the many improvements training will elicit.

Thanks to easy running, your body will also see an uptick in the enzymes that help to burn fat. Every cell in your body contains these enzymes, which sit waiting to be "turned on" by aerobic activity. No pills or special surgeries are needed: This is simply your body's natural way of burning fat. These enzymes work by making it possible for fats to enter the bloodstream and then travel to the muscles to be used as fuel. With the help of the increased mitochondria and fat-burning enzymes, the body utilizes fat for a longer period of time, pushing back the wall and keeping you running longer.

Capillary development is another benefit of easy running. Since running requires a greater amount of blood to supply oxygen to your system, the number of capillaries within the exercising muscles increases with training. After a number of months of running, capillary beds, or networks, can increase by as much as 40 percent. It should also be noted that the slow-twitch fibers contain an extensive network of capillaries compared with the fast-twitch fibers, supplying those slower fibers with much more oxygen. As the density of capillaries increases throughout those muscles, a greater amount of oxygen is supplied in a more efficient manner to the muscles.

Easy running also results in a number of adaptations that happen outside the exercising muscle. As you know, your body requires more oxygen as workload increases. The way to deliver more oxygen to your system is to deliver more blood. With several months of training, much of it easy running, an athlete will experience an increase in hemoglobin, which carries oxygen, in addition to a 35–40 percent increase in plasma volume. This increased volume not only helps deliver oxygen, but also carries away the waste products that result from metabolic processes.

Easy running also creates certain structural changes to your physiological system that you'll find advantageous for good marathoning. But none of these adaptations make much difference if there isn't a good pump to move all of this blood and oxygen through the system. Just like skeletal muscle, the heart gets stronger with exercise. More specifically, the heart's left ventricle increases in size and thickness, providing a bigger chamber to pump more blood from the heart to the arterial system. This gives the heart a break, as it won't be required to beat as often to deliver the same amount of blood, regardless of rest or exercise intensity. If you compare your heart rate from the beginning of a training cycle to the end, you'll be surprised by how much lower it can be. Again, this means that your system is becoming more efficient.

Another major physiological adaptation comes from within the tendons of the running muscles. The body lands at a force several times the runner's body weight, and the faster you run the greater that force becomes. The resulting strain on tendons and joints, applied gradually through easy running, allows these tendons to slowly adapt to higher impact forces to later handle the greater demands of fast-paced running.

Collectively, the adaptations stimulated by easy running prompt a higher VO_2max, anaerobic threshold, and running economy. While fast anaerobic workouts provide little improvement in the muscles' aerobic capacity and endurance, high amounts of easy running can bump aerobic development upward by leaps and bounds. Whether you're looking to strengthen your heart, transport more oxygen to the working muscles, or simply want to be able to run longer at a certain pace, all signs point to including high amounts of easy running in your training.

Easy Running Guidelines

An easy run is usually defined as a run that lasts anywhere between 20 minutes and 2.5 hours at an intensity of 55–75 percent of VO_2max. Since most of us don't have the means to get VO_2max tested, the next best thing is to look at pace per mile. The plans call for easy runs to be paced 1–2 minutes slower than goal marathon pace. So if your goal marathon pace is 8 minutes per mile, then your easy pace would be 9–10 minutes per mile. While easy running is a necessary part of marathon training, be sure not to run too easy. If your pace is excessively slow, you are simply breaking down tendon and bone without any aerobic benefits. Refer to Table 6.3 for your specific guidelines.

Keep in mind that there is a time for "fast" easy runs (1 minute per mile slower than marathon pace) and "slow" easy runs (2 minutes per mile slower than marathon pace). Warm-ups and cooldowns are two instances when you will want to run on the slower end of the spectrum. Here the idea is to simply bridge the gap between no running and fast running, and vice versa. For warm-ups, we recommend starting out very slow and then working the pace up to the faster end of the spectrum. For cooldowns, we advise keeping these closer to the slower end of the spectrum. The day after an SOS workout is another time you may choose a pace on the slow side. For instance, if you have a long run on Sunday and a strength workout on Tuesday, then Monday should be easier to ensure you are recovered and ready to run a good workout on Tuesday. By keeping the easy runs closer to 2 minutes per mile slower than marathon pace, beginning runners will safely make the transition to higher mileage. More advanced runners will likely find that they can handle the faster side of the easy range, even after SOS workouts. The day following a tempo run and the second easy day prior to a long run both provide good chances to run closer to 1 minute per mile slower than marathon race pace.

Whether you are a novice or an experienced runner, stick to the plan when it comes to easy running. Have fun with easy days, allowing yourself to take in the scenery or enjoy a social run with friends. Meanwhile, know you'll be simultaneously racking up a laundry list of physiological benefits. What's more, after a nice, relaxed run, your body will be clamoring for a challenge, ready to tackle the next SOS workout.

A note for Just Finish followers: Your training plan consists solely of easy runs and long runs (discussed next). If your goal is simply crossing that finish line, you are probably less concerned about your time. That can make pinpointing an appropriate easy pace more challenging because you don't have as much data to work with. You'll have to do a bit of trial and error and run by feel. For instance, if you start out at a 10-minute-per-mile pace and that feels quite challenging, then back off to a slower speed for your easy days. This process is valuable not only because it teaches you to listen to your body, but also because it often reveals to runners that they are capable of more than they thought as they start to gain fitness.

IS FASTER BETTER?

When it comes to easy runs, some runners think "if fast is good, faster is better," but that's not always the case during marathon training. When the plan prescribes 1–2 minutes slower than your goal marathon pace for easy runs, we really mean 1–2 minutes slower. You can opt for the slower or faster end of that spectrum based on how you're feeling that day. The bottom line is your SOS days should be hard and your easy runs should be easy. If you force the faster end of the pace all the time, you greatly increase your chances of injury and burnout. Remember, part of the importance of easy run is that they allow you to gain aerobic benefits yet still recover from the SOS days you are doing. If you are running too fast on easy days—for instance running a minute or less faster per minute than goal pace when you're feeling tired—then you have eliminated the recovery aspect from the run and the run loses some of its benefit.

Something of Substance "SOS" Workouts

The Long Run

The long run garners more attention than any other component of marathon training. It has become a status symbol among runners in training, a measure by which one compares oneself against running counterparts. It is surprising, then, to discover that much of the existing advice on running long is misguided. After relatively low-mileage weeks, some training plans suggest backbreaking long runs that are more akin to running misadventures than productive training. A 20-mile long run at the end of a three-day-a-week running program can be both demoralizing and physically injurious. The long run has become a big question mark, something you aren't sure you'll survive, but you subject yourself to the suffering nonetheless. Despite plenty of anecdotal and academic evidence against such training tactics, advice to reach (or go beyond) the 20-mile long run has persisted. It has become the magic number for marathoners, without consideration for individual differences in abilities and goals. While countless marathoners have made it to the finish line using these programs, we come to the table with a different approach. Not only will it make training more enjoyable, it will also help you cover 26.2 more efficiently.

While our long-run approach may sound radical, it is deeply rooted in results from inside the lab and outside on the roads. As I read through the exercise-science literature, coached the elite squad with Kevin and Keith, and tested theories in my own training, I realized that revisions to long-held beliefs about marathon training, and in particular long runs, were necessary. As a result, a 16-mile long run is the longest training day for the standard Hansons program. But there's a catch: One of Kevin and Keith's favorite sayings about the long run is, "It's not like running the first 16 miles of the marathon, but the last 16 miles!" What they mean is that the training plan simulates the cumulative fatigue that is experienced during a marathon, without completely zapping your legs. Rather than spending the entire week recovering from the previous long run, you should be building a base for the forthcoming long effort.

Take a look at a week in the From Scratch plan, which includes a 16-mile Sunday long run (page 112, week 15). Leading up to it, you are to do a Strength SOS on Wednesday, an easier short run on Friday, and a longer easy run on Saturday. We don't give you a day completely off before a long run because recovery occurs on the easy running days. Since no single workout has totally diminished your energy stores and left your legs feeling wrecked, you'll feel the effects of fatigue accumulating over time. The plan allows for partial recovery, but is designed to keep you from feeling completely fresh going into a long run. Following the Sunday long run, you will have an easy day of running (or off day depending on schedule) on Monday and an SOS workout Wednesday. This may initially appear to be too much, but because your long run's pace and mileage are tailored to your ability and experience, less recovery is necessary.

The physiology of long runs

Long runs bring with them a long list of psychological and physiological benefits, many of which correlate with the profits of easy running. Mentally, long runs help you gradually build confidence as you increase your mileage from one week to the next. They help you develop the coping skills necessary to complete any endurance event. They also teach you how to persist even when you are not feeling 100 percent. Since you never know what is going to happen on marathon day, this can be a real asset. Most notable, however, are the physiological adaptations that occur as a result of long runs. Improved VO_2max, increased capillary growth, and a stronger heart are among the benefits. Long runs also help to train your body to utilize fat as fuel on a cellular level. By training your body to run long, you let it adapt and learn to store more glycogen, thereby allowing it to go farther before becoming exhausted.

In addition to improving the energy stores in your muscles, long runs also increase muscle strength. Although your body first exploits the slow-twitch muscle fibers during a long run, it eventually begins to recruit the fast-twitch fibers as the slow-twitch fibers fatigue. Without strength training, the only way to train those fast-twitch fibers is to run long enough to tire the slow-twitch fibers first. By strengthening all of the fibers, you'll avoid bonking on race day. By now the majority of these adaptations are probably starting to sound familiar. You'll get many of the same benefits that you get from easier works from long runs too.

Long run guidelines

Advice from renowned running coach Dr. Jack Daniels provides a basis for our long-run philosophy. He instructs runners never to exceed 25–30 percent of their weekly mileage in a long run, whether they are training for a 5K or a marathon. He adds that a 2.5–3-hour time limit should be enforced, suggesting that exceeding those guidelines offers no physiological benefit and may lead to overtraining, injuries, and burnout.

Dr. Dave Martin, running researcher at Georgia State University and a consultant to Team USA, goes one step further, recommending that long runs be between 90 minutes and 2 hours long. While he proposes 18–25-mile long runs for high-level marathoners, one must take into consideration that a runner of this caliber can finish a 25-mile run in less than 3 hours. This highlights the importance of accounting for a runner's long-run pace. Dr. Joe Vigil, a Team USA coach and scientist, further supports this notion, advising that long runs be increased gradually until the athlete hits 2–3 hours. Certainly a 25-mile run completed in less than 3 hours by an elite runner will provide different physiological adaptations than a 25-mile run that takes a less experienced runner 3.5 hours or more.

According to South African researcher and author Dr. Tim Noakes, a continual, easy-to-moderate run at 70–85 percent VO_2max that is sustained for 2 hours or more will lead to the greatest glycogen depletion. Exercise physiologist Dr. David Costill has also noted that a 2-hour bout of running reduces muscle glycogen by as much as 50 percent. While this rate of glycogen depletion is acceptable on race day, it is counterproductive in the middle of a training cycle, as it takes as long as 72 hours to bounce back. When you diminish those energy stores, you can end up benched by fatigue, missing out on important training, or training on tired legs and potentially hurting yourself. Instead of risking diminishing returns and prescribing an arbitrary 20-mile run, we look at percentage of mileage and total time spent running. While 16 miles is often the suggested maximum run, we are more concerned with determining your long run based on your weekly total mileage and your pace for that long run. It may sound unconventional, but you'll find that nothing we suggest is random; it is all firmly based in science with proven results.

It is widely accepted among coaches that long runs shouldn't exceed 25–30 percent of weekly mileage. Even so, that guideline gets lost in many marathon-training programs in the effort to cram in mileage. For instance, a beginning program that peaks at 40–50 miles per week and recommends a 20-mile long run is violating the cardinal rule. Although the epic journey is usually sandwiched between an easy day and a rest day, there is no getting around the fact that it accounts for around 50 percent of the runner's weekly mileage. Looking at Table 6.1, you can see how far your long run should be based on your total mileage for the week.

The numbers illustrate that marathon training is a significant undertaking and should not be approached with haphazard bravado. They also make apparent the fact that many training programs miss the mark on the long run. If you are a beginning or low-mileage runner, your long runs must be adjusted accordingly. What is right for an 80-mile-a-week runner is not right for one who puts in 40 miles a week.

In addition to running the optimal number of miles on each long run, you must also adhere to a certain pace to get the most benefit. Since we don't all cover the same distance in the same amount of time, it makes sense to adjust

TABLE 6.1 **LONG RUN BASED ON TRAINING VOLUME**

	25% of volume	30% of volume
40 miles/week	10 mi.	12 mi.
50 miles/week	12.5 mi.	15 mi.
60 miles/week	15 mi.	18 mi.
70 miles/week	17.5 mi.	21 mi.

a long run depending on how fast you'll be traveling. The research tells us that 2–3 hours is the optimal window for development in terms of long runs. Beyond that, muscle breakdown begins to occur. Look at Table 6.2 to see how long it takes to complete the 16- and 20-mile distances based on pace.

The table demonstrates that a runner covering 16 miles at a 7:00-minute pace will finish in just under 2 hours, while a runner traveling at an 11:00-minute pace will take nearly 3 hours to finish that same distance. It then becomes clear that anyone planning on running slower than a 9:00-minute pace should avoid the 20-mile trek. This is where the number 16 comes into play. Based on the mileage from the Hansons marathon programs, the 16-mile long run fits the bill on both percentage of weekly mileage and long-run total time.

Speed Workouts

With speed workouts, marathon training gets even more interesting. When we refer to speed training, we are talking about interval sessions, also called repeat workouts. Speed workouts require you to run multiple bouts of certain distances at high intensities with recovery between each. Not only does this type of training play a role in prompting some of the important physiological changes we already discussed, it also teaches your mind to handle harder

TABLE 6.2 **LONG RUN DURATIONS BASED ON PACE**

Pace (min./mile)	16 miles	20 miles
7:00	1 hr. 52 min.	2 hrs. 20 min.
8:00	2 hrs. 8 min.	2 hrs. 40 min.
9:00	2 hrs. 24 min.	3 hrs.
10:00	2 hrs. 40 min.	3 hrs. 20 min.
11:00	2 hrs. 56 min.	3 hrs. 40 min.
12:00	3 hrs. 12 min.	4 hrs.
13:00	3 hrs. 28 min.	4 hrs. 20 min.

work. While easy days are typically low pressure, speed workouts require you to put your game face on and come ready to push hard. Discipline is one of many benefits. While you may be able to complete an easy run the morning following a late night out on the town, if you want to get the most out of your speed work, you're going to need to eat a hearty dinner and hit the hay at a decent hour. Whatever you give up to execute these workouts, optimally, the training will give back to you tenfold. Every speed workout you complete is like money in the bank when it comes to resources on which you can draw during the most difficult moments of the marathon.

Many beginning marathoners have done little or no speed workouts in the form of repeats or intervals. Luckily, the speed workouts in our plans provide an introductory course on how to implement harder workouts, no matter what distance you are training for. As you learn how to properly execute speed work-outs, your training will be transformed from a somewhat aimless approach to fitness to a guided plan of attack. Speed workouts can also help you predict what you are capable of in the marathon. They prepare you to successfully race a shorter race, such as a 5K or 10K, and then plug that time into a race equivalency chart to determine your potential marathon time. (See Table 9.1, "Race Equivalency Chart.") Additionally, this can help to highlight weak areas so you can address them early on.

Advanced runners and novices: Don't neglect your speed training. As with the other types of workouts, speed training is an important part of constantly keeping your system on its toes, requiring it to adapt to changing workouts that vary in intensity and distance.

Physiology of speed workouts

The greatest beneficiaries of speed training are the working muscles. With speed sessions, not only do the slow-twitch fibers become maximally activated to provide aerobic energy, so too do the intermediate fibers. This forces the slow-twitch fibers to maximize their aerobic capacities, but when they fatigue, it also trains the intermediate fibers to step in. As a result of better muscle coordination, running economy also improves. Stimulated by everything from speed workouts to easy running, running economy is all about how

WHAT ABOUT LONG RUN PACE?

Paces for long runs vary depending on the training level of the runner. If your primary goal is just to finish the 26.2-mile distance, pace isn't as important. Your main objective with the long run is to be able to cover the ground at a pace you can maintain the entire way. For those who are interested in experimenting with pace, we recommend staying at the slower end of the spectrum of easy pace. That said, if the mileage and the workouts aren't completely new to you, then you can venture into that faster end of the easy pace spectrum.

efficiently your body utilizes oxygen at a certain pace. Remember, running economy is a better predictor of race performance than VO_2max, so improvements can have a great influence on marathon performance.

Another adaptation that occurs through speed work is the increased production of myoglobin. In fact, research tells us that the best way to develop myoglobin is through higher intensity running (above 80 percent VO_2max). Similar to the way hemoglobin carries oxygen to the blood, myoglobin helps transport oxygen to the muscles and then to the mitochondria. With its help, the increased demand for oxygen is met to match capillary delivery and the needs of the mitochondria.

Exercise at higher intensities can also increase anaerobic threshold. In short, the speed intervals provide a two-for-one ticket by developing the anaerobic threshold and VO_2max during the same workout. Finally, since speed sessions include high-intensity running near 100 percent VO_2max (but not over), glycogen stores are rapidly depleted. In fact, during these workouts glycogen is providing upward of 90 percent of the energy. This, in turn, forces the muscles to adapt and store more glycogen to be used later in workouts.

Speed guidelines

Speed segments of our training plans are located toward the beginning of the training block, while later portions are devoted to more marathon-specific workouts. When you consider our contentions about building fitness from the bottom up, this may seem counterintuitive. However, if speed workouts are executed at the right speeds, it makes sense to include them closer to the beginning of your training cycle. Why? Because the most race-specific work should be done closer to the race. If you are preparing for a 5K, then yes, speed should be closer to your race. But in the case of marathon prep, there is little purpose in doing fast repeats on a track to prepare for the feeling of being at 22 miles with 4 more to go. Also, putting speed work early in the program allows a runner to do some shorter races before transitioning into full-blown marathon-training mode.

As with other workouts, correct pacing in your speed workouts is essential. When many coaches discuss speed training, they are referring to work that is done at 100 percent VO_2max. In reality, when you run at 100 percent VO_2max pace, it can be maintained for only 3–8 minutes. (For beginners, 3 minutes is likely more realistic, while an elite miler may be able to continue for close to 8 minutes.) Running your speed workouts at or above 100 percent VO_2max causes the structural muscles to begin to break down and forces your system to rely largely on anaerobic sources. Not only does this overstress the anaerobic system, it doesn't allow for the positive aerobic adaptations you need to run a good marathon. Our marathon programs base speed work on 5K and 10K goal times and these races both last much longer than 3–8 minutes. Rather than being at 100 percent VO_2max, you're probably between 80 and 95 percent VO_2max when running these distances. At these intensities, you aren't running fast enough to create an onset of severe acidosis (a condition when the muscles have a low pH brought on by high levels of blood lactate). Unlike other plans, we instruct you to complete speed workouts at slightly less than 100 percent VO_2max pace to spur maximum physiological adaptations. If you go faster, gains are nullified and injuries probable.

The duration of the speed intervals is also important. Optimal duration lies between 2 and 8 minutes. If the duration is too short, the amount of time spent at optimal intensity is minimized and precious workout time wasted. However, if the duration is too long, lactic acid builds up and you are too tired to complete the workout at the desired pace. As a result, the duration of speed intervals should be adjusted to your ability and experience levels. For example, a 400-meter repeat workout, with each interval lasting around 2 minutes, may be the perfect fit for a beginner. Conversely, the same workout may take an advanced runner 25 percent less time to complete each 400-meter repeat, therefore resulting in fewer benefits.

Recovery is another key part of speed sessions, allowing you the rest you need to complete another interval. Guidelines for recovery generally state that rest should be between 50 and 100 percent of the repeat duration time. For instance, if the repeat is 2 minutes in duration, the recovery should be between 1 and 2 minutes. However, we tend to give beginners longer recovery time at the beginning of their speed sessions to sustain them through the workout. Remember, if you are too tired to jog the recovery interval, then you're running too hard. The session is designed to focus on accumulating time within the desired intensity range. If you run your repeats so hard that you aren't able to jog during your recovery time, you are unlikely to be able to run the next interval at the desired pace. In the end, these speed sessions should total 3 miles of running at that faster intensity, in addition to the warm-up, cooldown, and recovery periods. If you can't get through the intervals to hit 3 miles total, you're running too hard for your abilities and thereby missing out on developing the specific adaptations discussed.

Your speed sessions are provided in the programs that follow in Chapter 7. Note that these workouts start with lower-duration repeats and work up to longer-duration repeats. Once the top of the ladder is reached (from shortest to the longest duration workouts) you are free to do the workouts that are the best fit for your optimal development.

If you're new to speed work, we strongly encourage you to join a local running group. Coaches and runners that are more experienced can take the guesswork and intimidation out of those first speed workouts by showing you the ropes. Additionally, a local track will be your best friend during this phase, as it is marked, consistent, and flat.

Strength Workouts

After you've spent a number of weeks performing periodic speed sessions, your muscle fibers and physiological systems have adapted quite well and are now ready for more marathon-specific adaptations. When strength workouts are added to the schedule, the goal of training shifts from improving the VO_2max (along with anaerobic threshold) to maintaining the VO_2max and

DECODING SPEED WORKOUTS

2-mile WU 6 × 800 m @ 5K pace with 400-m jog recovery 2-mile CD

Veterans of the sport and those who ran high school or college track might understand this workout immediately. Those who have never done interval workouts might find it a foreign language. Let's break it down:

2-mile WU: 2 continuous miles of easy running to warm up the body and prepare it for the hard workout.

6 × 800 m @ 5K pace with 400-m jog recovery: You will run 800 meters (roughly a half mile) at your 5K goal pace, then, without stopping or walking, run 400 m (roughly a quarter mile) at an easy recovery jog. After the recovery jog, you'll run another 800 m at 5K pace, followed by another 400-m jog recovery. Repeat until you've run six 800-m segments at 5K pace.

2-mile CD: 2 continuous miles of easy running to cool down and shake out the legs after the hard workout.

preparing the body to handle the fatigue associated with marathon running. You'll notice that at the same time the strength segment begins, the tempo runs and the long runs become more significant. At this point, everything the runner is doing is solely focused on marathon preparation.

When we talk about strength workouts, we aren't referring to intense sessions in the weight room, pumping iron and flexing muscles. Strength workouts are runs that emphasize intensity, rather than volume, with the goal of stressing the aerobic system at a high level. While the speed sessions are designed to be short enough to avoid lactate accumulation, the strength sessions are meant to force the runner to adapt to running longer distances with moderate amounts of lactate accumulation.

The physiology of strength workouts

Over time, strength sessions improve anaerobic capacities, which will allow your body to tolerate higher levels of lactic acid and produce less of it at higher intensities. While your body may have shut down in response to the lactic acid buildup at the beginning of training, strength sessions help your muscles learn to work through the discomfort of lactic acid accumulation. Additionally, strength sessions help train your exercising muscles to get better at removing lactic acid, as well as contribute to improving your running economy and allowing you to use less oxygen at the same effort. Strength workouts also spur development of something physiologists call "fractional utilization of maximal capacity." In practical terms, this allows a person to run at a faster pace for a longer period of time, which leads to an increase in anaerobic threshold. For the marathon, this means that glycogen will be conserved, so you can maintain your optimal marathon pace longer and stave off fatigue.

These adaptations all begin with an increase in the size of the heart's ventricle chamber. During a strength workout, the heart is required to pump faster and with more force than during easier runs. While it is not being worked quite as hard as during a speed session, it works at a fairly high intensity for significantly longer. The result is a stronger heart muscle with a larger chamber area, which means an increased stroke volume. (The stroke volume is the amount of blood pumped from the left ventricle per beat.) The benefit of this is that more blood is sent to the exercising muscles, and more oxygen is delivered. In addition, strength workouts help to involve the intermediate muscle fibers, increasing their oxidative capacities. Within the muscles, less lactate ends up being produced at faster speeds, and the lactate that is produced is recycled back into usable fuel. The practical purpose of all this is that running faster paces, especially near anaerobic threshold, begins to feel easier, you become more economical, and your stamina increases.

Strength guidelines

For most runners, the strength repeats will fall somewhere between 60 and 80 percent of VO_2max, which will be slower than the speed sessions. However, while the speed sessions are relatively short with moderate recovery, the strength sessions are double the volume with much shorter relative recovery. Strength workouts are designed to be run 10 seconds per mile slower than goal marathon pace. If your goal marathon pace is 8 minutes per mile, then your strength pace will be 7:50 per mile. The faster the runner, the closer this corresponds to half-marathon pace, but for the novice, this pace is between goal marathon pace and half-marathon ability. Although this may not seem like a big increase in pace, take a look at overall marathon times and you'll see that it makes a significant difference. For example, if your goal pace is 8 minutes per mile, you will finish around 3:30. However, if you run 7:50 per mile, just 10 seconds faster per mile, you will finish in 3:25. This faster overall time brings along with it a large increase in lactic acid. Even though the strength workout may not feel hard from an intensity standpoint, the volume, coupled with short recovery periods, is enough to stimulate lactic acid accumulation and make way for positive adaptations.

Recovery is key to the success of your strength sessions. In order to maintain a certain level of lactic acid, the recovery distance is kept to a fraction of the repeat duration. For instance, the 6 × 1-mile strength workout calls for a recovery jog of a quarter mile between each interval. If the repeats are to be done at 8-minute pace, the quarter-mile jog will end up taking between 2:30 and 3:00 minutes, totaling less than 50 percent of the duration of the intervals. Since these are less intense intervals, you may be tempted to exceed the prescribed pace, but keep in mind that the adaptations you're looking for specifically occur at that speed, no faster.

Strength workouts cover a lot of ground. So when gearing up for these sessions, consider finding a marked bike path or loop to execute them. While a track can be used, the workouts can get monotonous and injury is more likely. Remember to always include 1.5 to 3 miles of warm-up and cooldown.

Tempo Workouts

Tempo workouts, a staple of all endurance training plans, have been defined in numerous ways. For our purposes, a tempo run is a marathon-pace run. These runs will help you get a feel for what it is like to run race pace through a variety of conditions. Over the course of training, your tempo runs will span a number of months, requiring you to maintain race pace through an assortment of challenges and circumstances.

Internalizing pace is one of the most difficult components of training for runners to learn. If you feel great at the start line and go out 30 seconds per mile faster than you planned, you'll likely hit the halfway point ready to throw in the towel. No significant marathon records have ever been set via a positive split (running the second half slower than the first half). Put simply, if you want to have a successful marathon performance, you are better off maintaining a steady pace throughout the entire race, rather than following the "fly and die" method. Tempo runs teach you an important skill: control. Even when the pace feels easy, tempo workouts train you to hold back and maintain. Additionally, tempo runs provide a great staging ground for experimenting with different fluids, gels, and other nutritionals. Since you'll be running at marathon pace, you will get a good idea of what your body can and cannot handle. The same goes for your gear. Use the tempo runs as dress rehearsals to try various shoes and outfits to determine what is most comfortable. Regardless of training, these things can make or break your race; tempo runs provide perfect opportunities to fine-tune your race-day plans.

The physiology of tempo workouts

In the same way that easy and long runs improve endurance, so do tempo workouts. Although tempo days are faster than easy days, they are well under anaerobic threshold and thus provide many of the same adaptations. The longer tempo runs also mimic the benefits of long runs since the aerobic system is worked in similar ways. Specifically, from a physiological standpoint, the tempo run has a great impact on running economy at your goal race pace. One of the most visible benefits of this is increased endurance throughout a long race.

The tempo run has many of the same benefits as the strength workout. Also, since it is slower than a strength session, it elicits more aerobic benefits, similar to the long run. With tempo runs, the ability to burn fat is very specific to the workouts. The intensity is just enough that the aerobic system is challenged to keep up, but it's slow enough that the mitochondria and supporting fibers can barely keep up.

Over time it is the tempo run that will dictate whether or not you have selected the right marathon goal. With speed and strength sessions, you can in one sense "fake" your way through as a result of the relatively short repeats and ensuing breaks in between. However, with a tempo run, there is no break. If you are struggling to hit the correct pace for long tempo runs, you might legitimately question whether you can hold that pace for an entire marathon.

Perhaps the greatest benefit that tempo runs offer is the opportunity to thoroughly learn your desired race pace through repetition. With time, your body figures out a way to internalize how that pace feels, eventually making it second nature. Knowing what that pace feels like in heat, cold, rain, snow, and wind is incredibly valuable on race day. When runners cannot tell if they are on pace or not, they tend to be off pace (usually too fast), setting their race up for unavoidable doom. Learning your pace and the feel of that pace can make the difference between a good race and bad race.

Tempo workout guidelines

In our plans, tempo runs are completed at goal marathon pace, and are labeled in the charts as Tempo/MP. For many other coaches, a tempo run is much shorter at paces closer to strength pace, but for our purposes, tempo and marathon pace are interchangeable. The pace should remain at goal pace. Never hammer a tempo run because it feels "easy." Not only are you compromising physiological gains, but you're also not learning to be patient and internalizing pace. It will take a good number of tempo workouts before you fully internalize the pace and can regulate your runs based on feel. What does change throughout training is the distance of these workouts. Tempo runs are progressive in length, adjusting every few weeks, increasing from 4 miles for a beginner and 5 miles for an advanced runner to 10 miles over the last few weeks of training. As an advanced runner begins to reach the heaviest mileage, the total volume of a tempo run, with a warm-up and cooldown, can tally 12–14 miles and approach 90 minutes or more.

With the long run looming after a tempo run, that 16-miler might look a lot tougher than perhaps it did initially. This is a prime example of how our training employs cumulative fatigue. Suddenly a fairly easy longer run mimics the last 16 miles of the marathon. Rather than sending you into it feeling fresh, we try to simulate those last miles of the marathon, and there's nothing like a tempo run to put a little fatigue in your legs.

How to Pace Workouts

To help you better understand the intensity at which you should be running during the various components of the training plan, check out Figure 6.2. The diagonal line represents a sample VO$_2$max of a runner. The first zone (Easy) on the left is for the easy running days and represents everything under the aerobic threshold. It is the largest, but also the slowest area. The next zone (L) is the long run and represents the fastest paces a per-

HOW SHOULD A TEMPO RUN FEEL?

This is a common question, especially as runners get into 9–10-mile tempo distances. Many expect them to feel easier by this point in training, and when they don't, they fear they are not fit or will be unable to race at their goal pace. The dreaded, "I've got to go 16 more miles at this pace?" creeps into their minds. Don't undermine yourself. The truth is, for most people, the pace may never feel really comfortable, but at the end you should feel like you could have gone a couple more miles. Take confidence in that, and have faith in the process.

son should run for the long run, but could also represent the fastest of easy days for beginners. The middle zone (T) denotes ideal tempo pace, and therefore, marathon goal pace. It is above aerobic threshold, but below anaerobic threshold. The strength zone (ST) represents the high end of the "lactate" section, as strength runs should fall just below anaerobic threshold. Finally, there is the speed zone (SP) that represents where speed workouts should fall, which is just below VO_2max for optimal development.

With this continuum in mind, it becomes clear why running faster than you're instructed to run compromises development. When you go too fast, not only do you miss out, but you also increase fatigue. The essential point is this: Paces are there for a specific reason, and while some runners feel that paces sometimes hold them back, in reality proper pacing is what will propel you forward in the end. Fight the temptation to buy into the "if some is good, more is better" mentality and keep in mind the specific goal of that particular workout.

The Taper

Although we aren't generally in the business of telling folks to run less, cutting mileage and intensity is actually an integral part of marathon training when scheduled at the right times. For instance, while you may feel tired from the increased training two months into the program, avoid taking a day off and cutting your mileage that week. That is the wrong time, as it interferes with the foundational element of cumulative fatigue. However, when you reach the final stretch of training, your goal is to recover from all that work you put in, while also maintaining the improvements you made over the past few months. This is the right time to taper, or reduce your training volume, and it's one of the key steps in good marathoning.

The mistake many runners make with their tapering period is that they cut everything from training, including mileage, workouts, intensity, and easy days. In the same way that we instruct you not to add these components too soon, we also suggest not abruptly cutting them out. When runners subtract too much training too quickly, they often feel sluggish and even more fatigued than they did when they were in their peak training days. There's nothing worse than going into an important race feeling more tired than you did during training, and a proper taper is the key to avoiding this. By cutting the training back in a gradual manner, you'll feel fresh and ready to race.

An SOS workout takes about 10 days to demonstrate any physiological improvement. That's right: It takes more than a week before you reap any benefits from a hard run. If you look at the training plans in this book, you'll notice that the last SOS workout is done 10 days prior to the marathon, because after that point, SOS workouts will do nothing but make you tired on the big day. We also implement roughly a 55 percent reduction in overall volume the last seven days of the programs. You will still run the same number of days per week, but with daily mileage reduced. Why the same number of days? Kevin and Keith liken it to being used to getting six hours of sleep every night and then suddenly getting 12 hours. You will feel pretty groggy the next

FIGURE 6.2 **PACE VERSUS INTENSITY**

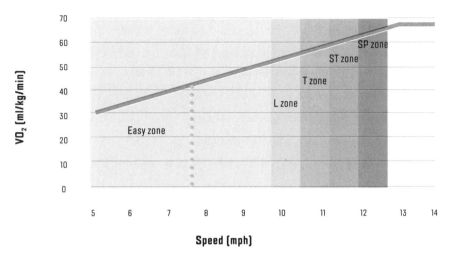

The speed at which you are running dictates which zone you are in.

day, even though you're well rested. The same can be said for being accustomed to running six days a week and then abruptly going down to only three or four days. It's a shock to the body. By continuing to run fewer miles, but still running every day, you reduce the number of variables that are adjusted. Instead of reducing frequency, volume, and intensity, you are tinkering only with the last two. Many other marathon training plans not only cut too much out of the schedule, but they also prescribe a taper of two to four weeks, causing a runner to lose some of those hard-earned fitness gains. By reducing the taper to just a 10-day period, you cut down on the risk of losing any of those gains, while still allowing adequate time for rest and recovery.

From a physiological standpoint, the taper fits well with the principle of cumulative fatigue, as the training program does not allow you to completely recover until you reach those final 10 days. Over the last couple months of the program, some of the good hormones, enzymes and functions in your body have been suppressed through incomplete recovery, while the by-products of fatigue have simultaneously been building. With reduced intensity and volume during the taper, these good functions flourish. Meanwhile, the by-products are allowed to completely break down and the body is left in a state of readiness for your best performance. We always warn runners not to underestimate the power of the taper. If you are worried about your ability to run a complete marathon at the pace of your tempo runs, consider this: The taper can elicit improvements of up to 3 percent. That is the difference between a 4:00 marathon and a 3:53 marathon. I don't know about you, but I'd be happy with a 7-minute improvement on my personal best.

Training Intensity Chart

To be used in determining how fast to run your workouts, Table 6.3 demonstrates pace per mile based on various goal marathon times. For easy runs, refer to the Easy Aerobic A and Easy Aerobic B columns. Keep in mind that actual 5K and 10K race times are going to be more accurate than this chart. If you have raced those distances, use your finishing times to guide your speed workouts. Our goal here is to provide you with guidance in your workouts, to help keep you focused and make the correct physiological adaptations throughout training.

TABLE 6.3 **TRAINING PACES**

Goal marathon time	Recovery	Easy aerobic A	Easy aerobic B	Moderate aerobic	Marathon pace (MP/ tempo)	Strength	Speed/ 10K
7:00:00	>18:31	18:31	17:31	17:01	16:01	15:51	14:41
6:45:00	>17:56	17:56	16:56	16:26	15:26	15:16	14:10
6:30:00	>17:22	17:22	16:22	15:52	14:52	14:42	13:38
6:15:00	>16:48	16:48	15:48	15:18	14:18	14:08	13:07
6:00:00	>16:13	16:13	15:13	14:43	13:43	13:33	12:35
5:45:00	>15:39	15:39	14:39	14:09	13:09	12:59	12:04
5:30:00	>15:05	15:05	14:05	13:35	12:35	12:25	11:32
5:15:00	>14:30	14:30	13:30	13:00	12:00	11:50	11:01
5:00:00	14:22	13:32	12:41	12:16	11:27	11:17	10:30
4:45:00	13:43	12:55	12:05	11:41	10:52	10:42	9:58
4:30:00	13:02	12:16	11:28	11:05	10:18	10:08	9:27
4:15:00	12:22	11:38	10:52	10:29	9:44	9:34	8:55
4:00:00	11:42	11:00	10:15	9:53	9:09	8:59	8:24
3:50:00	11:15	10:34	9:51	9:29	8:46	8:36	8:03
3:45:00	11:01	10:21	9:39	9:18	8:35	8:25	7:52
3:40:00	10:48	10:08	9:27	9:06	8:23	8:13	7:42
3:35:00	10:34	9:55	9:14	8:53	8:12	8:02	7:31
3:30:00	10:19	9:41	9:02	8:42	8:01	7:51	7:21
3:25:00	10:06	9:28	8:49	8:29	7:49	7:39	7:10
3:20:00	9:53	9:16	8:38	8:18	7:38	7:28	7:00
3:15:00	9:38	9:02	8:25	8:05	7:26	7:16	6:49
3:10:00	9:25	8:49	8:13	7:54	7:15	7:05	6:39
3:05:00	9:11	8:36	8:01	7:42	7:03	6:53	6:28
3:00:00	8:57	8:23	7:48	7:29	6:52	6:42	6:18
2:55:00	8:43	8:10	7:36	7:17	6:40	6:30	6:07
2:50:00	8:28	7:56	7:23	7:05	6:29	6:19	5:57
2:45:00	8:15	7:43	7:11	6:53	6:18	6:08	5:46
2:40:00	8:00	7:30	6:58	6:41	6:06	5:56	5:36
2:35:00	7:46	7:17	6:46	6:29	5:55	5:45	5:25
2:30:00	7:32	7:03	6:34	6:17	5:43	5:33	5:15
2:25:00	7:18	6:50	6:21	6:05	5:32	5:22	5:04
2:20:00	7:03	6:36	6:08	5:52	5:20	5:10	4:54
2:15:00	6:49	6:23	5:56	5:40	5:09	4:59	4:43
2:10:00	6:35	6:09	5:43	5:28	4:57	4:47	4:33

——— USING THE TRAINING PACES CHART ———

Find your goal marathon time. Follow the row across to see the recommended paces for all workouts—from easy runs to your speed SOS pace. All paces are minutes per mile.

Recovery: This is typically a pace you can run on a day when you need to recover. This can be your cooldown after an SOS day or even the day after an SOS day. You will still get aerobic training benefits from it. For most people, especially those training for 4 hours or more, the recovery paces probably won't be used because your easy pace is usually manageable.

Easy A and Easy B: This is a range, not an either or. Easy days, warm-ups, cooldowns, and long runs will typically fall into this range.

Moderate aerobic: More experienced runners can use this pace for easy runs and long runs if they are feeling good. However, there is no requirement to hit this pace.

Marathon: All SOS days labeled Tempo or MP will use this pace. This is your goal marathon race pace.

Strength: For any run labeled strength ("MP-10"), this is your goal marathon pace minus 10 seconds per mile.

Speed/10K: For any run labeled as speed or 10K pace, this column provides the pace for those SOS days.

HEART RATE TRAINING

We don't prescribe workouts based on heart rate. We're not against heart rate (HR); rather we are in favor of treating all methods, from GPS devices to strength training to heart rate to shoes, as mere tools. Focusing too much on any one tool can throw off the balance in your training. Yes, heart rate training can have a place in your training—just not a primary one on your speed, strength, tempo, and possibly your long runs. There, pacing calls the shots.

With our training, pace, not heart rate, is key. Why? Because the entire system is based on a goal and/or race pace. In our system, easy runs are based on an amount of time slower than goal marathon pace, tempo runs are based on goal pace, and strength workouts are a set amount faster than that goal pace. Many runners have a time goal in mind. It may be a Boston Qualifier, a sub-4:00, or an Olympic Trials qualifier. To run the pace required to meet your time goal becomes incredibly important. If you can't run those paces, then you can't reach your goal. So is it more important that you know you've kept your heart rate at 75 percent or that you have run the 8-minute-per-mile pace you need for a BQ? Let me just say, I haven't heard too many people cry out in joy at the finish line, "Yes! I kept my heart rate under 150!"

That said, if you feel HR training is the way to go, then here are a few tips.

Know your max heart rate. Have it tested (a VO$_2$max test), and get the HR ranges for your thresholds. The old standby equation to find HRmax (220 minus your age) is sufficient when looking at a large sample of people, but its individual accuracy can be questionable. Testing eliminates some of the guesswork.

Use all your tools. For example, GPS watches with HR monitors make this easy. Consider your tempo run. If you plan to run 8-minute miles, then it is helpful to know what your heart rate tends to be for those runs. If you see that heart rate

Continues

HEART RATE TRAINING [CONTINUED]

trend climbing, take note. Are you sick? Maybe it's something; maybe it's not. Use all the tools you have at hand—including your instincts—to know if you are training too hard. By relying on only one piece of data, you are at the mercy of all kinds of variables. Consider the whole picture. The main reasons we use heart rate are to gauge intensity and to monitor overtraining. Regarding these, does heart rate provide useful information? Potentially, but it's more useful in terms of tracking trends than in day-to-day numbers. If you use it, consider using it to help monitor your paces and see if you are getting fit enough to race at the pace you want to. Should you wear a monitor every day? I don't recommend that, nor do I recommend wearing a GPS every day. We know that new runners face a lot of unknowns: Am I too fast? Too slow? What exactly is too fast or slow? Am I improving? These are legitimate questions. Having something to measure and provide feedback is great. However, don't let that reliance keep you from learning to listen to what your body is telling you.

7

TRAINING PLANS

YOU'VE SPENT TIME doing the necessary soul-searching and number crunching to set your goal. It's important to keep those things in mind as you choose your training plan. Selecting the right plan is just as important as setting the right goal. For first-timers, we are big proponents of keeping it simple. To that end you'll find that we've narrowed your choices by distilling the options down to four training plans, in addition to the 0–5K program.

Be sure to look over each plan description, as well as the schedules themselves, to get a feel for your choices. After familiarizing themselves with all of the options, most runners find that one of the schedules jumps out as the right one. You've done plenty of reflection on the logistics of training to set your goals, so go with your gut on this.

— THE —
COUCH TO
MARATHON
PLAN
(WITH 0–5K PROGRAM)

Couch to Marathon (C2THON)

If you're starting from ground zero in terms of running experience and fitness, then this is the smartest way to safely go from no running to the 26.2-mile race. Before you begin to think about running a marathon, you should be running at least 30 minutes, five days a week. From there, you can move forward with the marathon-specific program that fits you best. The first section of the C2THON program—called the 0–5K plan— also gives you the opportunity to run a 5K race and thereby establish a baseline for your marathon training if you struggled to pinpoint a goal time.

Notice in the 0–5K schedule schedule that you don't go straight from zero to 30 minutes of running. The plan eases you into the mileage to help avoid injuries and burnout. On Day 1, for instance, your total workout is scheduled for 30 minutes; however, that time frame is broken down into a warm-up, a run/walk workout, and a cooldown. So your total running time is actually only 5 minutes.

— THE —
0-5K
PLAN

0 to 5K

Notice that at the end of this 8-week program, there is a 30-minute run scheduled on the final Saturday. This would be a perfect opportunity to run a 5K race to establish a baseline. From there, you can use a race equivalency calculator to get an idea of what your starting paces should be for marathon training. (We provide a comprehensive interactive calculator at http:bit.ly/2t8w3pd.)

Once you've completed the 0–5K plan, you're ready to transition into a marathon training plan. Be conservative about your marathon plan choice. Our From Scratch or Just Finish plans are likely the most suitable. Each is described in more detail in the pages that follow. Choose the one that is most suitable for your marathon journey.

Note: The following list reflects the info in the training plan that immediately follows; see Monday, week 1, in that plan/table.

HERE'S HOW DAY 1 BREAKS DOWN:

10 Minutes: Warm-Up Walk

Start at a comfortable pace, increasing to a brisk speed over the last few minutes.

10 Minutes: Run/Walk Sequence

Alternate jogging 1 minute at a comfortable pace and then walking 1 minute, for a total 5 minutes of jogging and 5 minutes of walking. The walk can be at whatever pace will allow you to complete the jogging portions. Experiment to establish the right pace. A mistake people often make is running the early jog portions too fast and then slowing down considerably or needing a break towards the end. Repeat this sequence 5 times:

> 1-minute jog
> 1-minute walk
> 1-minute jog
> 1-minute walk
> 1-minute jog
> 1-minute walk
> 1-minute jog
> 1-minute walk
> 1-minute jog
> 1-minute walk

10 Minutes: Cooldown Walk

This helps bring your heart rate down, but still plays a role in cardio-vascular development and building endurance.

0–5K

WEEK	MONDAY	TUESDAY	WEDNESDAY	THURSDAY
1	10 min. walk		10 min. walk	
	5 sets of: 1 min. walk 1 min. jog	Rest or crosstrain	5 sets of: 1 min. walk 1 min. jog	Rest or crosstrain
	10 min. walk		10 min. walk	
	30 min.		30 min.	
2	9 min. walk		9 min. walk	
	4 sets of: 1 min. walk 2 min. jog	Rest or crosstrain	4 sets of: 1 min. walk 2 min. jog	Rest or crosstrain
	9 min. walk		9 min. walk	
	30 min.		30 min.	
3	7 min. walk		7 min. walk	
	4 sets of: 1 min. walk 3 min. jog	Rest or crosstrain	4 sets of: 1 min. walk 3 min. jog	Rest or crosstrain
	7 min. walk		7 min. walk	
	30 min.		30 min.	
4	4 min. walk		4 min. walk	
	4 sets of: 1 min. walk 5 min. jog	Rest or crosstrain	3 sets of: 1 min. walk 7 min. jog	Rest or crosstrain
	2 min. walk		2 min. walk	
	30 min.		30 min.	
5	5 min. walk		5 min. walk	
	3 sets of: 1 min. walk 8 min. jog	Rest or crosstrain	2 sets of: 1 min. walk 10 min. jog	Rest or crosstrain
	3 min. walk		3 min. walk	
	35 min.		30 min.	

O–5K

FRIDAY	SATURDAY	SUNDAY	WEEKLY TOTAL
10 min. walk	10 min. walk		
5 sets of: 1 min. walk 1 min. jog	5 sets of: 1 min. walk 1 min. jog	Rest or crosstrain	
10 min. walk	10 min. walk		
30 min.	30 min.		2 hrs.
9 min. walk	9 min. walk		
4 sets of: 1 min. walk 2 min. jog	4 sets of: 1 min. walk 2 min. jog	Rest or crosstrain	
9 min. walk	9 min. walk		
30 min.	30 min.		2 hrs.
7 min. walk	8 min. walk		
4 sets of: 1 min. walk 3 min. jog	4 sets of: 1 min. walk 2.5 min. run	Rest or crosstrain	
7 min. walk	8 min. walk		
30 min.	30 min.		2 hrs.
4 min. walk	5 min. walk		
4 sets of: 1 min. walk 5 min. jog	4 sets of: 1 min. walk 4 min. jog	Rest or crosstrain	
2 min. walk	5 min. walk		
30 min.	30 min.		2 hrs.
5 min. walk	5 min. walk		
3 sets of: 1 min. walk 8 min. jog	4 sets of: 1 min. walk 6 min. jog	Rest or crosstrain	
3 min. walk	2 min. walk		
35 min.	35 min.		2 hrs. 15 min.

0–5K

Continues

0-5K (CONTINUED)

WEEK	MONDAY	TUESDAY	WEDNESDAY	THURSDAY
6	5 min. walk		4 min. walk	
	2 sets of: 1 min. walk 10 min. jog	Rest or crosstrain	2 sets of: 1 min. walk 15 min. jog	Rest or crosstrain
	3 min. walk		4 min. walk	
	30 min.		40 min.	
7	5 min. walk		5 min. walk	
	20 min. jog	Rest or crosstrain	25 min. jog	Rest or crosstrain
	5 min. walk		5 min. walk	
	30 min.		35 min.	
8	5 min. walk		5 min. walk	
	30 min. jog	Rest or crosstrain	30 min. jog	Rest or crosstrain
	5 min. walk		5 min. walk	
	40 min.		40 min.	

0-5K

FRIDAY	SATURDAY	SUNDAY	WEEKLY TOTAL
5 min. walk	5 min. walk		
2 sets of: 1 min. walk 10 min. jog	2 sets of: 1 min. walk 10 min. jog	Rest or crosstrain	
3 min. walk	3 min. walk		
30 min.	30 min.		2 hrs. 10 min.
5 min. walk	4 min. walk		
20 min. jog	2 sets of: 1 min. walk 15 min. jog	Rest or crosstrain	
5 min. walk	4 min. walk		
30 min.	40 min.		2 hrs. 15 min.
5 min. walk	5 min. walk		
30 min. jog	30 min. jog Congrats!	Rest or crosstrain	
5 min. walk	5 min. walk		
40 min.	40 min.		2 hrs. 40 min.

0–5K

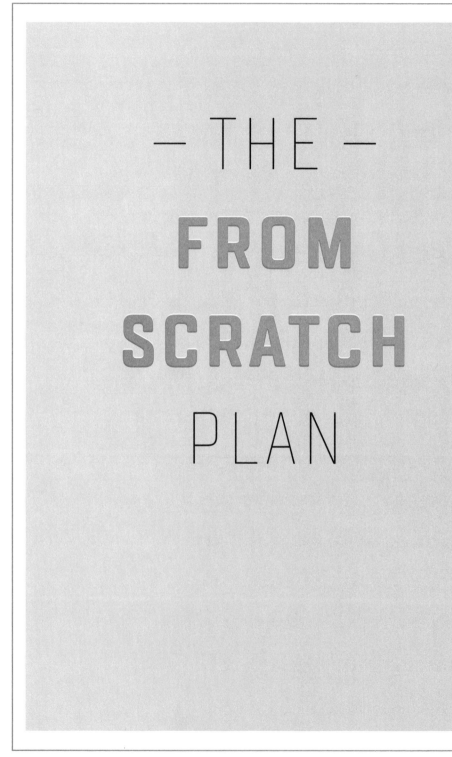

— THE —

FROM
SCRATCH
PLAN

From Scratch Plan

If you followed the first part of our C2THON program, the 8-week 0–5K program, then you can transition directly into this plan. This plan is also excellent for those who are already currently running 10–15 miles per week.

The From Scratch plan is a great fit for the runner who is fairly new to the sport and wants to learn more about how to do all the marathon workouts beyond just long runs. If you choose this program, you'll get an introduction to our Something of Substance (SOS) days. These are workouts where we vary intensity, teach you how to run different paces, and educate you on tempo runs and speed workouts. Note: If you're looking to simply finish the race, then you may prefer to skip this section and proceed to the Just Finish program.

This plan starts with a weekly total of 17 miles and builds to a peak of 46 miles. That might seem like a big jump, but remember that you will be taking your time to build strength, endurance, and mileage over many weeks. In this program, you are called to do two SOS days per week as the schedule progresses. Couple those two days with two off days and this schedule lays out a calculated plan to build your fitness safely and effectively without overtraining you.

FROM SCRATCH 18 WEEK / 5 DAYS PER WEEK BEGINNER PROGRAM

WEEK	MONDAY	TUESDAY	WEDNESDAY	THURSDAY
1	3 mi. easy	3 mi. easy	Off: Crosstrain/ strength OK	3 mi. easy
	3 mi.	3 mi.		3 mi.
2	4 mi. easy	4 mi. easy	Off: Crosstrain/ strength OK	4 mi. easy
	4 mi.	4 mi.		4 mi.
3	4 mi. easy	5 mi. easy	Off: Crosstrain/ strength OK	5 mi. easy
	4 mi.	5 mi.		5 mi.
4	4 mi. easy	1.5 mi. warm-up 6 × 800m at goal MP w/ 400m jog recovery 1.5 mi. cooldown	Off: Crosstrain/ strength OK	5 mi. easy
	4 mi.	7.5 mi.		5 mi.
5	4 mi. easy	1.5 mi. warm-up 4 × 1 mi. @ goal MP w/ 400m jog recovery 1.5 mi. cooldown	Off: Crosstrain/ strength OK	6 mi. easy
	4 mi.	8 mi.		6 mi.

TEMPO

FRIDAY	SATURDAY	SUNDAY	WEEKLY TOTAL
3 mi. easy	Off: Crosstrain/ strength OK	5 mi. easy	
3 mi.		5 mi.	17 mi.
Off: Crosstrain/ strength OK	4 mi. easy	6 mi. easy	
	4 mi.	6 mi.	22 mi.
Off: Crosstrain/ strength OK	4 mi. easy	8 mi. easy	
	4 mi.	8 mi.	26 mi.
Off: Crosstrain/ strength OK	5 mi. easy	10 mi. long	
	5 mi.	10 mi.	31.5 mi.
Off: Crosstrain/ strength OK	6 mi. easy	10 mi. long	
	6 mi.	10 mi.	34 mi.

Continues

FROM SCRATCH

FROM SCRATCH [CONTINUED]

WEEK	MONDAY	TUESDAY	WEDNESDAY	THURSDAY
6	4 mi. easy	Off: Crosstrain/ strength OK	1.5 mi. warm-up 12 × 400m @ 10K pace w/ 400m jog recovery 1.5 mi. cooldown	6 mi. easy
	4 mi		9 mi.	6 mi.
7	4 mi. easy	Off: Crosstrain/ strength OK	1.5 mi. warm-up 6 × 800m @ 10K pace w/ 400m jog recovery 1.5 mi. cooldown	6 mi. easy
	4 mi		7.5 mi.	6 mi.
8	Off: Crosstrain/ strength OK	6 mi. easy	1.5 mi. warm-up 5 × 1K @ 10K pace w/ 400m jog recovery 1.5 mi. cooldown	Off: Crosstrain/ strength OK
		6 mi.	7 mi.	
9	Off: Crosstrain/ strength OK	6 mi. easy	1.5 mi. warm-up 4 × 1200m @ 10K pace w/ 400m jog recovery 1.5 mi. cooldown	Off: Crosstrain/ strength OK
		6 mi.	7 mi.	

FROM SCRATCH

SPEED

FRIDAY	SATURDAY	SUNDAY		WEEKLY TOTAL
Off: Crosstrain/ strength OK	6 mi. easy	1.5 mi. warm-up 4 miles @ goal MP 1.5 mi. cooldown	TEMPO	
	6 mi.	7 mi.		32 mi.
Off: Crosstrain/ strength OK	6 mi. easy	12 mi. long		
	6 mi.	12 mi.		35.5 mi.
Off: Crosstrain/ strength OK	8 mi. easy	1.5 mi. warm-up 8 miles @ goal MP 1.5 mi. cooldown	TEMPO	
	8 mi.	11 mi.		32 mi.
4 mi. easy	8 mi. easy	14 mi. long		
4 mi	8 mi.	14 mi.		39 mi.

FROM SCRATCH

Continues

FROM SCRATCH (CONTINUED)

WEEK	MONDAY	TUESDAY	WEDNESDAY	THURSDAY
10	Off: Crosstrain/ strength OK	6 mi. easy	1.5 mi. warm-up 6 × 800m @ 10K pace w/ 400m jog recovery 1.5 mi. cooldown SPEED	Off: Crosstrain/ strength OK
		6 mi.	7.5 mi.	
11	Off: Crosstrain/ strength OK	6 mi. easy	1.5 mi. warm-up 6 × 1 mi. @ goal MP-10 sec/mi. w/ 400m jog recovery 1.5 mi. cooldown STRENGTH	Off: Crosstrain/ strength OK
		6 mi.	10.5 mi.	
12	Off: Crosstrain/ strength OK	6 mi. easy	1.5 mi. warm-up 4 × 1.5 mi. @ goal MP-10 sec/mi. w/ 0.5 mi. jog 1.5 mi. cooldown STRENGTH	Off: Crosstrain/ strength OK
		6 mi.	11 mi.	
13	Off: Crosstrain/ strength OK	6 mi. easy	1.5 mi. warm-up 3 × 2 mi. @ goal MP-10 sec./mi. w/ 0.5 mi. jog recovery 1.5 mi. cooldown STRENGTH	Off: Crosstrain/ strength OK
		6 mi.	10.5 mi.	

FROM SCRATCH

FRIDAY	SATURDAY	SUNDAY		WEEKLY TOTAL
4 mi. easy	8 mi. easy	1.5 mi. warm-up 8 miles @ goal MP 1.5 mi. cooldown	TEMPO	
4 mi	8 mi.	11 mi.		36.5 mi.
4 mi. easy	10 mi. easy	16 mi. long		
4 mi	10 mi.	16 mi.		46.5 mi.
6 mi. easy	8 mi. easy	1.5 mi. warm-up 10 mi. @ goal MP 1.5 mi. cooldown	TEMPO	
6 mi.	8 mi.	13 mi.		44 mi.
4 mi. easy	10 mi. easy	16 mi. long		
4 mi	10 mi.	16 mi.		46.5 mi.

FROM SCRATCH

Continues

FROM SCRATCH (CONTINUED)

WEEK	MONDAY	TUESDAY	WEDNESDAY		THURSDAY
14	Off: Crosstrain/ strength OK	6 mi. easy	1.5 mi. warm-up 2 × 3 mi. @ goal MP-10 sec./mi. w/ 1 mi. jog recovery 1.5 mi. cooldown	STRENGTH	Off: Crosstrain/ strength OK
		6 mi.	11 mi.		
15	Off: Crosstrain/ strength OK	6 mi. easy	1.5 mi. warm-up 3 × 2 mi. @ goal MP-10 sec./mi. w/ 0.5 mi. jog recovery 1.5 mi. cooldown	STRENGTH	Off: Crosstrain/ strength OK
		6 mi.	10.5 mi.		
16	Off: Crosstrain/ strength OK	6 mi. easy	1.5 mi. warm-up 4 × 1.5 mi. @ goal MP-10 sec./mi. w/ 0.5 mi. jog recovery 1.5 mi. cooldown	STRENGTH	Off: Crosstrain/ strength OK
		6 mi.	11 mi.		

FROM SCRATCH

FRIDAY	SATURDAY	SUNDAY		WEEKLY TOTAL
6 mi. easy	8 mi. easy	1.5 mi. warm-up 10 mi. @ goal MP 1.5 mi. cooldown	TEMPO	
6 mi.	8 mi.	13 mi.		44 mi.
4 mi. easy	10 mi. easy	16 mi. long		
4 mi	10 mi.	16 mi.		46.5 mi.
6 mi. easy	8 mi. easy	1.5 mi. warm-up 10 mi. @ goal MP 1.5 mi. cooldown	TEMPO	
6 mi.	8 mi.	13 mi.		44 mi.

Continues

FROM SCRATCH

FROM SCRATCH (CONTINUED)

WEEK	MONDAY	TUESDAY	WEDNESDAY	THURSDAY
17	Off: Crosstrain/ strength OK	6 mi. easy	1.5 mi. warm-up 6 × 1 mi. @ goal MP-10 sec./mi. w/ 400m jog recovery 1.5 mi. cooldown	Off: Crosstrain/ strength OK
		6 mi.	10.5 mi.	STRENGTH
18	Off: Crosstrain/ strength OK	6 mi. easy	1.5 mi. warm-up 3 × 2 min. @ MP w/ 2 min. jog recovery 3 × 2 mi. @ goal MP-10 sec./mi. w/ 0.5 mi. jog recovery 1.5 mi. cooldown	Off: Crosstrain/ strength OK
		6 mi.	17 mi.	TEMPO

FROM SCRATCH

FRIDAY	SATURDAY	SUNDAY	WEEKLY TOTAL
4 mi. easy	6 mi. easy	12 mi. long	
4 mi	6 mi.	12 mi.	38.5 mi.
4 mi. easy	Easy 30 min. shakeout	Race day!	
4 mi	3 mi.	26.2	56.2 mi.

— THE —
JUST FINISH PLAN

The Just Finish Plan

If you picked up this book in hopes of simply finishing your first marathon, our Just Finish plan is for you. It is perfect for runners who have the itch to complete a marathon but are not interested in or perhaps not ready at this time for the "extra stuff" (i.e., SOS days). This plan will prepare you to finish strong and cross the marathon off your bucket list.

Just as in the From Scratch plan, the total weekly mileage of the Just Finish plan tops out at about 45 miles per week during peak training, and you will still run 6 days per week. This is because even if your goal is simply to finish, running 26.2 miles still requires a solid amount of training in order to adequately and safely complete that distance on race day.

At first blush, that kind of mileage might sound pretty daunting. Rather than focusing on that peak number, instead just focus on Week 1, which totals only 12 miles. Take confidence in knowing that the plan will build up your mileage over a number of weeks, so what might feel impossible now will feel far more possible and doable down the line.

Keep in mind that without the SOS days, the mileage will feel easier to tolerate and you'll recover more quickly. Simply focus on completing the prescribed distance each day and avoid running faster than what is called for. Intensity, not mileage, is the biggest training killer for the majority of runners we've worked with. By eliminating the variable of high-intensity workouts, you can still build the strength and endurance to finish a marathon. We will cover more specifics about intensity and pace in the coming pages.

JUST FINISH 18 WEEK / 6 DAYS PER WEEK PROGRAM

WEEK	MONDAY	TUESDAY	WEDNESDAY	THURSDAY
1	Rest or crosstrain	2 mi. easy	Rest or crosstrain	3 mi. easy
2	Rest or crosstrain	3 mi. easy	Rest or crosstrain	3 mi. easy
3	Rest or crosstrain	4 mi. easy	Rest or crosstrain	4 mi. easy
4	Rest or crosstrain	5 mi. easy	Rest or crosstrain	3 mi. easy
5	Rest or crosstrain	5 mi. easy	Rest or crosstrain	4 mi. easy
6	4 mi. easy	5 mi. easy	Rest or crosstrain	5 mi. easy
7	4 mi. easy	6 mi. easy	Rest or crosstrain	5 mi. easy
8	6 mi. easy	5 mi. easy	Rest or crosstrain	6 mi. easy
9	5 mi. easy	6 mi. easy	Rest or crosstrain	5 mi. easy
10	7 mi. easy	5 mi. easy	Rest or crosstrain	6 mi. easy
11	5 mi. easy	7 mi. easy	Rest or crosstrain	5 mi. easy

JUST FINISH

FRIDAY	SATURDAY	SUNDAY	WEEKLY TOTAL
Rest or crosstrain	3 mi. easy	4 mi. easy	12 mi.
3 mi. easy	3 mi. easy	4 mi. easy	16 mi.
4 mi. easy	4 mi. easy	5 mi. easy	21 mi.
3 mi. easy	5 mi. easy	4 mi. easy	20 mi.
5 mi. easy	4 mi. easy	6 mi. easy	24 mi.
4 mi. easy	8 mi. easy	8 mi. easy	34 mi.
4 mi. easy	6 mi. easy	10 mi. long run	35 mi.
5 mi. easy	6 mi. easy	10 mi. long run	38 mi.
6 mi. easy	5 mi. easy	15 mi. long run	42 mi.
5 mi. easy	8 mi. easy	10 mi. long run	41 mi.
6 mi. easy	8 mi. easy	16 mi. long run	47 mi.

JUST FINISH

Continues

JUST FINISH

JUST FINISH (CONTINUED)				
WEEK	MONDAY	TUESDAY	WEDNESDAY	THURSDAY
12	5 mi. easy	7 mi. easy	Rest or crosstrain	6 mi. easy
13	7 mi. easy	5 mi. easy	Rest or crosstrain	5 mi. easy
14	5 mi. easy	7 mi. easy	Rest or crosstrain	6 mi. easy
15	7 mi. easy	5 mi. easy	Rest or crosstrain	5 mi. easy
16	5 mi. easy	5 mi. easy	Rest or crosstrain	5 mi. easy
17	7 mi. easy	5 mi. easy	Rest or crosstrain	5 mi. easy
18	5 mi. easy	5 mi. easy	Rest	5 mi. easy

FRIDAY	SATURDAY	SUNDAY	WEEKLY TOTAL
5 mi. easy	8 mi. easy	10 mi. long run	41 mi.
6 mi. easy	6 mi. easy	16 mi. long run	45 mi.
5 mi. easy	8 mi. easy	10 mi. long run	41 mi.
6 mi. easy	6 mi. easy	16 mi. long run	45 mi.
5 mi. easy	8 mi. easy	10 mi. long run	38 mi.
6 mi. easy	6 mi. easy	8 mi. easy	37 mi.
4 mi. easy	3 mi. easy	Race day! 26.2 mi.	48.2 mi.

JUST FINISH

— THE —

ADVANCED

FIRST

TIMER

PLAN

Advanced First Timer Plan

This plan is designed for the runner who is experienced in other running events up to the half-marathon and is accustomed to training 5–6 days and 50–60 miles per week. The plan emphasizes more weekly volume sooner than the other schedules, while still allowing for adequate rest between hard workouts.

Even the best runners can struggle with week after week of marathon training. Because of that, this plan strategically spaces out your SOS workouts, sometimes breaking them up with a medium-length long run during the week to give your body more time to recover. This schedule stays true to the philosophy behind our traditional Hansons Marathon Method plans, with a few tweaks. Those tweaks act as a safety valve, designed to prevent you from overtraining by giving you a less intense week every second week. Since optimal sleep, nutrition, and stretching aren't always achievable in real-world scenarios, these tweaks offer a little extra recovery on a regular basis to keep you up and running.

ADVANCED FIRST TIMER 18 WEEK PROGRAM

WEEK	MONDAY	TUESDAY	WEDNESDAY	THURSDAY
1	6 mi. easy	6 mi. easy	Off: Crosstrain/ strength OK	6 mi. easy
	6 mi.	6 mi.		6 mi.
2	6 mi. easy	6 mi. easy	Off: Crosstrain/ strength OK	1.5 mi. warm-up 6 × 800m @ goal MP w/ 400m jog recovery 1.5 mi. cooldown **TEMPO**
	6 mi.	6 mi.		7.5 mi.
3	4 mi. easy	1.5 mi. warm-up 12 × 400m @ 10K pace w/ 400m jog recovery 1.5 mi. cooldown **SPEED**	Off: Crosstrain/ strength OK	6 mi. easy
	4 mi.	9 mi.		6 mi.
4	4 mi. easy	1.5 mi. warm-up 8 × 600m @ 10K pace w/ 400m jog recovery 1.5 mi. cooldown **SPEED**	Off: Crosstrain/ strength OK	6 mi. easy
	4 mi.	8 mi.		6 mi.

FRIDAY	SATURDAY	SUNDAY	WEEKLY TOTAL
6 mi. easy	Off: Crosstrain/ strength OK	6 mi. easy	
6 mi.		6 mi.	30 mi.
4 mi. easy	4 mi. easy	8 mi. long	
4 mi.	4 mi.	8 mi.	35.5 mi.
6 mi. easy	4 mi. easy	10 mi. long	
6 mi.	4 mi.	10 mi.	39 mi.
1.5 mi. warm-up 4 × 1 mi. @ goal MP w/ 400m jog recovery 1.5 mi. cooldown **TEMPO**	6 mi. easy	8 mi. long	
8 mi.	6 mi.	8 mi.	40 mi.

Continues

ADVANCED FIRST TIMER (CONTINUED)

WEEK	MONDAY	TUESDAY		WEDNESDAY	THURSDAY	
5	6 mi. easy	1.5 mi. warm-up 6 × 800m @ 10K pace w/ 400m jog recovery 1.5 mi. cooldown	SPEED	Off: Crosstrain/ strength OK	1.5 mi. warm-up 2 × 2 mi. @ goal MP with 0.5 mi. jog recovery 1.5 mi. cooldown	TEMPO
	6 mi.	7.5 mi.			7.5 mi.	
6	6 mi. easy	1.5 mi. warm-up 5 × 1K @ 10K pace w/ 400m jog recovery 1.5 mi. cooldown	SPEED	Off: Crosstrain/ strength OK	8 mi. easy	
	6 mi.	7 mi.			8 mi.	
7	6 mi. easy	1.5 mi. warm-up 4 × 1200m @ 10K pace w/ 400m jog recovery 1.5 mi. cooldown	SPEED	Off: Crosstrain/ strength OK	1.5 mi. warm-up 3 mi.-2mi.-1 mi. @ goal MP w/ 0.5 mi. jog recovery 1 mi. cooldown	TEMPO
	6 mi.	7 mi.			10 mi.	
8	6 mi. easy	1.5 mi. warm-up 4 × 1 mi. @ MP -10 sec. w/ 400m jog recovery 1.5 mi. cooldown	SPEED	Off: Crosstrain/ strength OK	1.5 mi. warm-up 2 × 3 mi. @ goal MP with 1 mi. jog recovery 1.5 mi. cooldown	
	6 mi.	8 mi.			10 mi.	

ADVANCED FIRST TIMER

FRIDAY	SATURDAY	SUNDAY		WEEKLY TOTAL
6 mi. easy	6 mi. easy	10 mi. long		
6 mi.	6 mi.	10 mi.		43 mi.
6 mi. easy	6 mi. easy	2 mi. warm-up 6 mi. @ goal MP 2 mi. cooldown	TEMPO	
6 mi.	6 mi.	10 mi.		43 mi.
4 mi. easy	6 mi. easy	10 mi. long		
4 mi.	6 mi.	10 mi.		43 mi.
4 mi. easy	8 mi. easy	14 mi. long		
4 mi.	8 mi.	14 mi.		50 mi.

Continues

ADVANCED FIRST TIMER

ADVANCED FIRST TIMER (CONTINUED)

WEEK	MONDAY	TUESDAY		WEDNESDAY	THURSDAY
9	6 mi. easy	1.5 mi. warm-up 4 × 1 mi. @ MP −10 sec. w/ 400m jog recovery 1.5 mi. cooldown	STRENGTH	Off: Crosstrain/ strength OK	1.5 mi. warm-up 2 × 3 mi. @ goal MP with 1 mi. jog recovery 1.5 mi. cooldown
	6 mi.	8 mi.			10 mi.
10	6 mi. easy	1.5 mi. warm-up 4 × 1.5 mi. @ MP −10 sec./mi. w/ 0.5 mi. jog recovery 1.5 mi. cooldown	STRENGTH	Off: Crosstrain/ strength OK	10 mi. long
	6 mi.	11 mi.			10 mi.
11	6 mi. easy	1.5 mi. warm-up 6 × 1 mi. @ MP −10 sec./mi. w/ 400m jog recovery 1.5 mi. cooldown	STRENGTH	Off: Crosstrain/ strength OK	1.5 mi. warm-up 2 mi.-3 mi. -2 mi. @ goal MP w/ 0.5 mi. jog recovery 1.5 mi. cooldown
	6 mi.	10.5 mi.			11 mi.
12	6 mi. easy	1.5 mi. warm-up 3 × 2 mi. @ MP −10 sec./mi. w/ 0.5 mi. jog recovery 1.5 mi. cooldown	STRENGTH	Off: Crosstrain/ strength OK	12 mi. med.-long
	6 mi.	10.5 mi.			12 mi.

FRIDAY	SATURDAY	SUNDAY		WEEKLY TOTAL
4 mi. easy	8 mi. easy	14 mi. long		
4 mi.	8 mi.	14 mi.		50 mi.
6 mi. easy	8 mi. easy	2 mi. warm-up 8 mi. @ goal MP 2 mi. cooldown	TEMPO	
6 mi.	8 mi.	12 mi.		53 mi.
4 mi. easy	10 mi. easy	16 mi. long		
4 mi.	10 mi.	16 mi.		57.5 mi.
6 mi. easy	8 mi. easy	1.5 mi. warm-up 10 mi. @ goal MP 1.5 mi. cooldown	TEMPO	
6 mi.	8 mi.	13 mi.		55.5 mi.

ADVANCED FIRST TIMER

Continues

ADVANCED FIRST TIMER (CONTINUED)

WEEK	MONDAY	TUESDAY		WEDNESDAY	THURSDAY
13	6 mi. easy	1.5 mi. warm-up 3 mi.-2 mi.-1 mi. @ MP-10 sec./mi. w/ 0.5 mi. jog recovery 1.5 mi. cooldown	STRENGTH	Off: Crosstrain/strength OK	1.5 mi. warm-up 2 × 4 mi. @ goal MP w/ 1 mi. jog recovery 1.5 mi. cooldown
	6 mi.	10.5 mi.			13 mi.
14	6 mi. easy	1.5 mi. warm-up 3 × 2 mi. @ MP-10 sec./mi. w/ 0.5 mi. jog recovery 1.5 mi. cooldown	STRENGTH	Off: Crosstrain/strength OK	12 mi. med.-long
	6 mi.	10.5 mi.			12 mi.
15	6 mi. easy	1.5 mi. warm-up 6 × 800m @ 10K pace w/ 400m jog recovery 1.5 mi. cooldown	SPEED	Off: Crosstrain/strength OK	1.5 mi. warm-up 3 mi -2 mi.-3 mi. @ goal MP w/ 0.5 mi. jog recovery 1.5 mi. cooldown
	6 mi.	7.5 mi.			12.5 mi.
16	6 mi. easy	1.5 mi. warm-up 2 × 3 mi. @ MP-10 sec./mi. w/ 1 mi. jog recovery 1.5 mi. cooldown	STRENGTH	Off: Crosstrain/strength OK	12 mi. med.-long
	6 mi.	11 mi.			12 mi.

ADVANCED FIRST TIMER

FRIDAY	SATURDAY	SUNDAY		WEEKLY TOTAL
6 mi. easy	10 mi. easy	16 mi. long		
6 mi.	10 mi.	16 mi.		61.5 mi.
6 mi. easy	8 mi. easy	1.5 mi. warm-up 10 mi. @ goal MP 1.5 mi. cooldown	TEMPO	
6 mi.	8 mi.	13 mi.		55.5 mi.
6 mi. easy	10 mi. easy	16 mi. long		
6 mi.	10 mi.	16 mi.		58 mi.
6 mi. easy	8 mi. easy	1.5 mi. warm-up 10 mi. @ goal MP 1.5 mi. cooldown	TEMPO	
6 mi.	8 mi.	13 mi.		56 mi.

Continues

ADVANCED FIRST TIMER

ADVANCED FIRST TIMER (CONTINUED)

WEEK	MONDAY	TUESDAY	WEDNESDAY		THURSDAY
17	4 mi. easy	6 mi. easy	1.5 mi. warm-up 6 × 1 mi. @ goal MP-10 sec./mi. w/ 400m jog recovery 1.5 mi. cooldown	STRENGTH	Off: Crosstrain/ strength OK
	4 mi.	6 mi.	10.5 mi.		
18	4 mi. easy	6 mi. easy	1.5 mi. warm-up 8 mi. easy w/ 3 × 2 min. @ MP w/ 2 min. jog recovery 1.5 mi. cooldown	TEMPO	Off: Crosstrain/ strength OK
	4 mi.	6 mi.	11 mi.		

FRIDAY	SATURDAY	SUNDAY	WEEKLY TOTAL
4 mi. easy	6 mi. easy	12 mi. long	
4 mi.	6 mi.	12 mi.	42.5 mi.
4 mi. easy	30 min.easy shakeout	Race day!	
4 mi.	3 mi.	26.2 mi.	54.2 mi.

— THE —
EXPRESS
PLAN

Express Plan

This highly focused training plan is specifically built for runners who have just come off a racing segment. A good candidate for this plan would be someone who, for example, just completed the summer racing circuit for a local run club and is now turning his or her attention to a fall marathon. This training plan will help you switch gears from focusing on speed to instead investing your efforts into marathon-specific work. As a result of your previous training and fitness, we can safely put you into a two-month dedicated block of race-specific work that won't drag on forever and end up overcooking you.

Peruse all your training plan options, and then choose the plan that offers the best match with your current fitness, as well as your desires and goals. Following that plan to the letter is the most assured way to reach your goal, but you might find, thanks to family and work commitments, that it's not always realistic. It's important to explore the potential modifications you can make to these plans when life gets in the way of training. Chapter 8 explains how to deal with hiccups in training without getting totally derailed.

EXPRESS PLAN 12 WEEK PROGRAM

WEEK	MONDAY	TUESDAY	WEDDAY	THURSDAY
1	4 mi. easy	6 mi. easy	Off: Crosstrain OK	1 mi. warm-up 5 × 1 mi. MP w/ 400m jog recovery 1 mi. cooldown
	4 mi.	6 mi.		8 mi.
2	5 mi. easy	6 mi. easy	Off: Crosstrain OK	1 mi. warm-up 2 × 2 mi. MP with 0.5 mi. jog recovery 1 mi. cooldown
	5 mi.	6 mi.		7 mi.
3	6 mi. easy	1.5 mi. warm-up 6 × 800m @ 10K pace w/ 400m jog recovery 1.5 mi. cooldown — SPEED	Off: Crosstrain OK	1 mi. warm-up 5 mi. @ MP 1 mi. cooldown — TEMPO
	6 mi.	7.5 mi.		7 mi.
4	5 mi. easy	1.5 mi. warm-up 4 × 1.5 mi. @ MP -10 sec. w/ 800m jog recovery 1.5 mi. cooldown — STRENGTH	Off: Crosstrain OK	1.5 mi. warm-up 6 mi. @l MP 1.5 mi. cooldown — TEMPO
	5 mi.	11 mi.		9 mi.

EXPRESS

FRIDAY	SATURDAY	SUNDAY	WEEKLY TOTAL
4 mi. easy	8 mi. easy	10 mi. long	
4 mi.	8 mi.	10 mi.	40 mi.
6 mi. easy	8 mi. easy	12 mi. long	
6 mi.	8 mi.	12 mi.	44 mi.
6 mi. easy	8 mi. easy	14 mi. long	
6 mi.	8 mi.	14 mi.	48.5 mi.
5 mi. easy	10 mi. easy	16 mi. long	
5 mi.	10 mi.	16 mi.	56 mi.

Continues

EXPRESS

EXPRESS PLAN (CONTINUED)

WEEK	MONDAY	TUESDAY		WEDNESDAY	THURSDAY	
5	8 mi. easy	1.5 mi. warm-up 6 × 800m @ 10K pace w/ 400m jog recovery 1.5 mi. cooldown	SPEED	Off: Crosstrain OK	1.5 mi. warm-up 6 mi. @ MP 1.5 mi. cooldown	TEMPO
	8 mi.	7.5 mi.			9 mi.	
6	6 mi. easy	2 mi. warm-up 3 × 2 mi. @ MP -10 sec. w/ 800m jog recovery 2 mi. cooldown	STRENGTH	Off: Crosstrain OK	1.5 mi. warm-up 8 mi. @ MP 1.5 mi. cooldown	TEMPO
	6 mi.	11.5 mi.			11 mi.	
7	8 mi. easy	1.5 mi. warm-up 5 × 1K @ 10K pace w/ 400m jog recovery 1.5 mi. cooldown	SPEED	Off: Crosstrain OK	1.5 mi. warm-up 2 × 5 mi. @ MP w/ 1 mi. jog recovery 1.5 mi. cooldown	TEMPO
	8 mi.	7 mi.			14 mi.	
8	6 mi. easy	1.5 mi. warm-up 2 × 3 mi. @ MP -10 sec. w/ 1 mi. jog recovery 1.5 mi. cooldown	STRENGTH	Off: Crosstrain OK	1.5 mi. warm-up 10 mi. @ MP 1.5 mi. cooldown	TEMPO
	6 mi.	11 mi.			13 mi.	

EXPRESS

FRIDAY	SATURDAY	SUNDAY	WEEKLY TOTAL
6 mi. easy	8 mi. easy	14 mi. long	
6 mi.	8 mi.	14 mi.	52.5 mi.
6 mi. easy	10 mi. easy	16 mi. long	
6 mi.	10 mi.	16 mi.	60.5 mi.
6 mi. easy	8 mi. easy	14 mi. long	
6 mi.	8 mi.	14 mi.	58 mi.
6 mi. easy	10 mi. easy	16 mi. long	
6 mi.	10 mi.	16 mi.	62 mi.

EXPRESS

Continues

EXPRESS PLAN (CONTINUED)

WEEK	MONDAY	TUESDAY	WEDNESDAY	THURSDAY	
9	6 mi. easy	2 mi. warm-up 3 × 2 mi. @ MP -10 sec. w/ 800m jog recovery 2 mi. cooldown	Off: Crosstrain OK	2 mi. warm-up 2 × 5 mi. @ MP w/ 1 mi. jog recovery 2 mi. cooldown	TEMPO
	6 mi.	11.5 mi.		15 mi.	
10	6 mi. easy	1.5 mi. warm-up 4 × 1.5 mi. @ goal MP w/ .5 mi. jog recovery 1.5 mi. cooldown	STRENGTH / Off: Crosstrain OK	1.5 mi. warm-up 8 mi. @ MP 1.5 mi. cooldown	TEMPO
	6 mi.	11 mi.		11 mi.	
11	4 mi. easy	1.5 mi. warm-up 6 × 800 @ 10K pace w/ .25 mi. jog recovery 1.5 mi. cooldown	Off: Crosstrain OK	1.5 mi. warm-up 6 mi. @ MP 1.5 mi. cooldown	TEMPO
	4 mi.	7.5 mi.		9 mi.	
12	6 mi. easy	1.5 mi. warm-up 6 mi. easy w/ 3 × 2 min. @ MP w/ 2 min. jog recovery 1.5 mi. cooldown	Off: Crosstrain OK	6 mi. easy	
	6 mi.	9 mi.		6 mi.	

EXPRESS

FRIDAY	SATURDAY	SUNDAY	WEEKLY TOTAL
6 mi. easy	8 mi. easy	14 mi. long	
6 mi.	8 mi.	14 mi.	60.5 mi.
6 mi. easy	10 mi. easy	16 mi. long	
6 mi.	10 mi.	16 mi.	60 mi.
4 mi. easy	4 mi. easy	12 mi. long	
4 mi.	4 mi.	12 mi.	40.5 mi.
4 mi. easy	3 mi. easy shakeout run	Race day!	
4 mi.	3 mi.	26.2 mi.	54.2 mi.

EXPRESS

8

MODIFYING
YOUR PLAN

IN A PERFECT WORLD, you would select your training plan and then follow it all the way through, to the letter, for the best running experience of your life. In reality, however, even with the best intentions, training doesn't always go according to plan. As such, view your training plan as a best-case scenario. As coaches, runners, spouses, parents, and employers ourselves, we know that all sorts of hurdles can get thrown your way and interrupt training. The key is not letting those setbacks derail you. Slightly modifying the plan is always better than bailing on your training and goals altogether. Missing a day or even a week of training, whether for a family emergency, illness, or unexpected work trip, doesn't signal a need to hit the eject button. The goal of this chapter is to show you how to take a schedule and make it work with the unpredictabilities of everyday life.

Making modifications to a marathon plan can be a bit more complicated than a 5K or 10K plan. Keep in mind: The longer the distance, the more vital things like consistency and rest become. In the end, the unique situation you're in will dictate your best course. However, when it comes to modification, there are some general guidelines that apply in all circumstances. Let's look at those.

Guideline 1: Maintain Regularity in Training

Aim for regularity and consistency in training. Missing a day here or there is not a big deal, but when skipping days becomes a regular practice, it may signal that training has slipped down on your priority list. It is still possible to train for a marathon, but you'll have to adjust your expectations.

Consider, too, the role that motivation is playing in driving your training. When we're motivated, things seem to work like clockwork, we get our training in, and we feel like we're conquering the world. Of course, not every day feels like that. But low motivation on a particular day doesn't mean that you should skip a workout. For example, if Thursday is your tempo day, then do your best to keep it on Thursday, rather than put it off to another day in the hopes that you'll feel more motivated to get it done. Over time, those little changes erode the integrity of the training plan as well as your overall commitment. Get 'er done!

Guideline 2: Ensure Rest Days and Easy Days Remain in Place

Always take either an easy day or a rest day between SOS workouts. This allows for proper recovery. If you miss your speed workout on Tuesday and complete it on Wednesday instead, and then go right into your tempo run on Thursday, you're asking for an injury. In this situation, your best bet is to move the tempo run to Friday, leaving an easy run on Saturday and a long run on Sunday. This way, you are adjusting for obligations and disruptions without upsetting the entire balance of training.

Guideline 3: Something Is Always Better Than Nothing

Consider the previous example, where an SOS workout was missed on Tuesday. What's a runner to do if there is no other possible day to reschedule the workout later in the week? One option is to just move on. That's right: Cut your losses and move on to the next SOS workout. In some circumstances, there may be no way around this scenario. If you don't have time to get in the full workout, however, consider sneaking in a quick run or abbreviate the workout and get in what you can. Even a 25-minute run is better than skipping a workout altogether.

Now let's dive a little deeper. Events that force athletes to modify training tend to fall into six general categories. These include the following:

One-offs: random events such as a doctor's appointment.

Consistent unavailability: a scheduled event that always falls on an SOS day. For instance, your kid's swim practice is always on Tuesday, the same day as your Tuesday SOS.

Consistent inconsistency: Your weeks are unpredictable, often due to work. For example, business travelers often know they will be gone, but might not know details until a week or few days before.

A race: A race affects your training in the days before the race, the day of the race, and several days following. It's important to know when a race is a good idea and how to adjust accordingly.

Minor illness or injury: This may cause you to miss 3–5 days.

Significant illness or injury: This may cause you to take 7 or more days off in a row.

One-Off Events

Sometimes life intervenes and throws off our daily routines. Your car breaks down and you end up skipping your run. Your child gets sick and you have to scrap your workout. This is likely to happen at least once or twice during a marathon cycle. In most of these situations, it's best to just pick up wherever you left off the next day. For instance, if you had to take Wednesday off for an eye exam, but have a tempo run on Thursday, then pick up with the tempo on Thursday. There is no need to make that Wednesday up. Now, if you have an off day again later in the week, perhaps you do an easy run to recoup some of that lost mileage. Some people add to their other runs—a little bit here and a little bit there—to gradually add back some of their lost mileage. This is perfectly OK too, although not entirely necessary.

If you took a day off because you had a niggle or were sick, that's another story. We will discuss injury and illness in depth on the following pages, but it's worth mentioning here that in these types of circumstances, your next run back shouldn't be an SOS run. It should be an easy run. You can pick back up with the schedule after that if you're feeling 100 percent.

Consistent Unavailability

You picked your training plan, and immediately noticed that one of the weekly days on the running schedule is not going to work with your life schedule. For instance, some athletes want to take Sunday completely off, either for religious reasons or as dedicated family time. You can adjust for that. In most situations, it's a matter of a simple (consistent) switch or a shift in days. In the Sundays-off example, you could shift your long run to Saturday, and then switch out the easy day that was originally on Saturday with the regularly scheduled off day, thereby moving the off day to Sunday. Now, you may have only one day off or an easy day between workouts, so you'll need to pay extra attention to how you approach each SOS day and subsequent recovery, but that might be a good thing because it'll force you to be conservative on those runs! The key here is flexibility coupled with consistency.

Consistent Inconsistency

This is a common stumbling block for business travelers. They might have a "normal" schedule for two weeks, and then suddenly they are off on a cross-country trip for three days. While tricky, this is not an excuse to take three days off. But it does force you to get creative. You may find yourself switching days around or scaling things back. No, this is not ideal, and it may cause you to reassess your goal time. But trust us, it can be manageable. Just remember to adjust what you are realistically able to and get in whatever training is possible. If this goal is important enough to you, there will always be a way.

Races

One of the most common reasons runners require a change in their training program is to accommodate races. While we suggest including other races sparingly leading up to a marathon, in certain instances they definitely offer advantages. For example, we have discussed the benefits of a beginner racing a 5K or 10K to help establish a baseline for marathon-specific training.

Furthermore, for those with little to no racing experience, it's useful to gain familiarity with a race atmosphere before marathon day. This allows you to practice your pre-race routine so it all feels like old hat when you get to the big 26.2.

While useful, lead-up races must be strategically scheduled. The best time to schedule a race depends on the program you're following.

From Scratch: This plan offers two good opportunities to race progressively longer races without impacting your overall training. The first, at the end of Week 5, presents a good opening to run a 10K. By Week 5, you know you can run 3 miles, so a 10K will provide a little better comparison point if you are trying to settle on a marathon goal.

Adjusting for this race is simple: Let's assume the 10K is on a Saturday. You can scrap your 10-mile long run on that Sunday and insert Saturday's 6-mile run in its place. Then on Saturday, run your 10K race hard, and include a 2-mile warm-up and a 2-mile cooldown. Right there you've done the 10-mile run that you are missing on Sunday, so your weekly mileage doesn't take a hit. Furthermore, you will then have three consecutive off or easy days before your next SOS day. This allows plenty of time to recover, yet still lets you get mileage in.

A second prime opportunity is to race a half-marathon at the end of Week 10. If you adjusted your race goal and training paces based on your 10K performance in Week 5, a half-marathon 5 weeks later will be sufficient time to see a boost in fitness. More importantly, it gives you about 6.5 weeks to really dial in marathon fitness.

During the final 2 months of training, you will have your longest runs and be doing your most marathon-specific work, so it's best not to race during those 8 weeks.

Implementing a half-marathon race into your schedule is a little bit trickier than it was for the 10K. Assuming the race is on the Sunday of Week 10, do the following:

- Switch the Thursday off day to Friday

- Move the Saturday 8 miler to Thursday

- Move the Friday 4 miler to Saturday

- Instead of a longer tempo, Sunday is the race

As for how to race the half-marathon, we don't recommend running it as hard as you can. If you've chosen the From Scratch training plan, then 13.1 miles may well be the longest race you have ever run. Add to that the fact that you are not cutting back any training, just shifting it around, so it's best to tiptoe with caution into uncharted territory. If you are too aggressive with unrealistic expectations, then it's easy to have your confidence crushed. But if you ease into it and surprise yourself, then you can build on that momentum.

To approach the half-marathon with restraint, use the first 2 miles as your warm-up, gradually increasing your pace along the way. Treat the next 6 miles as a marathon-pace tempo run. This will get you to 8 miles, and here you can test the waters a little bit. If you aren't sure about yourself, keep the pace steady. If you have an itch to really see what you can do, try running the next 3 miles at 10–15 seconds per mile faster than your goal marathon pace. Finally, use last couple miles as a cooldown.

Remember, the objective for running this race isn't necessarily to adjust your marathon goal, although it should help solidify it, but rather, to create an opportunity to become familiar with running hard for a long way and having to control your emotions, keep pace in check, and learn patience. These are all vital components to success in a marathon.

Just Finish: Followers of this plan can run the same two races as those doing the From Scratch plan. Similarly, the 10K should be run at Week 5; however, you will need to move more components around. Assuming a Saturday 10K:

❯ Switch Thursday and Friday

❯ Take out Sunday's 6 miler

❯ Move Saturday's 4 miler to Sunday

❯ Race on Saturday with a 1-mile warm-up and 1-mile cooldown

For the Just Finish plan, your best opening to run a half-marathon race is Week 13. This week has a 16-mile long run, which will become your half-marathon—with a little adjustment. To make your half-marathon a 16-mile day, add a 1.5-mile warm-up before the race and a 1.5-mile cooldown after the race, or if you prefer, do a 3-mile warm-up before the race. This way you can go straight to the post-race relaxation and refreshments (the best part).

Doing a half-marathon race in Week 13 of your program provides an excellent opportunity to practice proper pacing, patience, and staying emotionally steady.

Advanced First Timer: Most runners following this plan have already run plenty of 10K races and maybe a few half-marathons as well, and therefore probably have plentiful experience with the race atmosphere. This also means there is less need to build up to progressively longer races. You will be better served by putting most of your energy into training. That said, doing a half-marathon at the end of Week 16 is a very useful idea. Week 16 serves as your last big week of training, and running a half-marathon race at that time allows you to stage a dress rehearsal for the marathon.

Here's how to implement a half-marathon race on the Sunday of Week 16:

❭ Switch Friday and Saturday around.

❭ Scale the Thursday 12 miler back to a 10 miler

❭ On Sunday, race day, keep the 1.5-mile warm-up and cooldown, and just add the 13.1-mile race in place of the scheduled tempo

❭ During the race, run the first 8–10 miles at goal marathon pace before deciding if it's a good idea to step on the gas

The objective of the half-marathon race is not to run a personal best, but rather, to be in a race atmosphere and practice controlling your pacing, being patient, and executing your fueling/hydration plan.

Running these less important races can provide great insight into your training if approached at the right times and with the right mindset. Races aren't a substitute for training, but a supplement to it. Remember, everything you do in your training plan should have a purpose and make a positive impact on the end goal, not take away from it. If you are following the Express Plan, your guidelines are the same as in the Advanced First Timer plan, so please refer to the information above.

Illness or Injury

Illness and injury are surely the most frustrating reasons you may need to adjust your marathon training. Over the months you spend preparing for the 26.2-mile distance, you are likely, at the very least, to catch a bug. The chance of injury, on the other hand, is largely avoided through smart training, although not entirely eliminated. Even when you're doing everything right, you can still trip on a curb and take a spill or roll an ankle on uneven terrain.

The first step in these circumstances is deciding if you need a day or two completely off or if you can modify the workout instead.

If pain is your issue, consider the following rules of thumb in making a determination:

> ❭ On a scale from zero to 10, how much pain are you in?
> If the pain is more than a 3, don't run.

> ❭ Are you limping during or following a run? Don't run.

> ❭ Do you need medication in order to run or to numb pain? Don't run.

With illness, the general rule of thumb is that if you have a fever, do not run. Focus on recovery instead. Running with a fever will ultimately set you back even further by delaying your body's ability to bounce back. But if you simply have a cold with a runny nose, then you are probably well enough to push through or modify what you do for the day.

Below is a general guide to help you modify the day's workout with an aim toward minimizing damage or loss of fitness. Choose the modification that suits your particular situation—one that will make things better, not worse. These modifications are listed on a sliding scale, from the smallest tweak to the schedule (a close variation of the actual workout) to the biggest change (total rest).

Do the full workout, but switch from a distance-based workout to a time-based workout to take some pressure off. For instance, instead of 10 × 400 meters with 400 meters rest, do 10 × 2 minutes on with 3 minutes off. Simply estimate how long it would have previously taken you to run the prescribed distance (i.e., 400 meters) and use that time for your repeats (i.e., 2 minutes).

Do the scheduled number of miles for the day, but modify the workout by either running at a slower pace or reducing the volume of hard running you do.

Do the scheduled number of miles for the day, but run it at an easy pace.

Reduce your mileage for the day and run easy.

Swap running with crosstraining and add some core work and resistance training. Opt for crosstraining that is as close to a replacement of running as possible (without aggravating an injury). The most popular tend to be elliptical, bicycling, and swimming. For more on core work and resistance training, visit Chapter 11, Supplemental Training, for specific suggestions.

Do only core work and resistance training. See Chapter 11 for more information on supplemental training. Do only what does not aggravate your injury.

Take the day off completely.

When we are faced with serious layoffs from training, the schedule may need to be adjusted (and worst-case scenario, goals abandoned). How you navigate these unfortunate layoffs will depend on their length.

You missed 1–2 days

From Scratch, Advanced First Timer, or Express runners: It's fairly easy to compensate for a few days missed due to a minor illness or niggle. You can resume normal training without scaling back mileage or intensity. You have lost only a couple of days of running; no harm done. For example, let's say you took a wrong step at the end of your long run on Sunday and twisted your ankle, causing you to miss training on Monday and Tuesday. You can simply jump back in on Wednesday. If you are feeling 100 percent, complete Tuesday's SOS workout on Wednesday and move the Thursday tempo to Friday. This allows you to still fit in all of the week's SOS workouts, but also adheres to the rule of scheduling an easy or rest day between hard runs. However, if you aren't able to reschedule your SOS days to fit within those parameters, then just forge ahead with your tempo run on Thursday and let go of the missed SOS workout. While a number of missed workouts can spell doom for your marathon goals, a single lost workout will never be your demise.

Just Finish runners: Missing 1 or 2 days will cause minimal (if any) setback. If you miss one day, just jump back into the schedule. For two days missed, scale that first run back by 1–2 miles and then proceed as the schedule dictates.

You missed 3–6 days

From Scratch, Advanced First Timer, or Express runners: Physiological regression will be minimal, even if no running at all takes place within this time frame. Usually, a person missing this many days has something more than a 24-hour flu or a simple ache or pain. If you are feeling healthy enough to get in a couple of short, easy jogs while you recuperate, by all means do it. However, if you're truly laid up, rest assured that the consequences of 3–6 days off won't affect your end goal. Come back slowly by running easy for 2–3 days, then pick the schedule back up and follow it as usual.

Just Finish runners: When you come back to training, scale back your first three runs by 25–30 percent, and then continue as originally scheduled. If 5–6 days are missed, run easy for 3–4 days, and then revert to the previous week's training regimen. After that week, jump ahead and catch back up with the training schedule. For instance, if you miss Week 3, run easy through Week 4, and then return to Week 3's plan during the fifth week. After that, jump to Week 6 and follow the training as it was originally prescribed.

You missed 7–10 days

Advanced First Timer, From Scratch, Express runners: At this point, your body starts to lose some of the hard-earned physiological gains you have made.

It always seems to take a lot more time and effort to gain fitness than it does to lose it. No running for a week and a half necessitates serious schedule modification; however, that modification depends upon at what point in the plan the missed block occurs. If it occurs before the strength portion of the training program, then you won't have to make any major adjustments to race goals. However, if the setback happens after the strength workouts begin, you'll probably need to adjust race-time goals for the following reasons: (1) There may not be time to get in all the prescribed training, and (2) the desired physiological adaptations might not have the necessary time to occur. Keep in mind that if you can still manage to do some short, easy runs during this period and have the go-ahead from your doctor, the time it takes to return to normal training will be significantly less. In either case, you don't need to completely abandon your plans to run the marathon, although adjustments are necessary.

Upon your return to training, you should run easy for the same number of days that were missed. If a week was lost, then run easy for a week. After that, go back to the last training week that you were able to complete and repeat it, then run the week that was originally missed, and from there pick the schedule back up. So with a week missed, it takes three weeks to get back on track. If you were able to run easy during your time off, subtract a week from that time frame. While this advice applies throughout the training program, once strength workouts have begun, you may do the math and realize, "Wow! I don't have enough time."

This is especially true with the Express plan, since we are working with only 12 weeks to begin with. While many people can still rebound quickly enough to run the race, the goal time will likely be compromised. Once you get into that final 4–6 weeks of training, the pros and cons of racing should be weighed. If you are looking to run a Boston qualifier and you miss 10 days of running with 5 weeks to go, you may choose to look at other, later race options to buy yourself time. If you are comfortable with potentially missing the mark, however, then go for it.

Just Finish: Take your last completed week and run 60 percent of that week's mileage upon returning to running. Then repeat your last completed scheduled week—so the week you ran at 60 percent will now be repeated, but at 100 percent effort. After that, jump back to where you were on the schedule.

You missed 11+ days (all plans)

If you are forced to miss this much time, you are faced with a serious decision, regardless of which program you followed. After two weeks of lost training, the decreases in physiological gains are significant—as much as 3–5 percent. While this might not seem like much, consider this: For a runner attempting a 3-hour marathon, a 4 percent loss means a gain of 7 minutes to the overall finishing time. The slower the marathon time, the more time lost. Even worse, after 21 days away from running, you have forfeited 10 percent or more of your fitness. This means that VO_2max and blood volume can decrease by up to 10 percent, anaerobic threshold decreases significantly, and muscle glycogen decreases by as much as 30 percent. These are all important to marathon performance, and if you miss two weeks of running, it may take more than two weeks to even get back to your pre-injury level, setting you far behind schedule. In particular, if this happens during the strength portion of the program, there simply may not be enough time to regain your fitness levels and get you ready for the goal race.

While you won't run your best, advanced runners in this situation may be able to sneak in shorter training segments and still complete the race, albeit falling short of the original time goal. However, beginners should be cautious when it comes to losing substantial amounts of training time and forging ahead to the goal race. For any runner in this situation, consider choosing a new race or at least revising time goals. In all of our years of coaching, we've seen too many people rush back from injury to make a race deadline, often leading them to forgo proper recovery and have a poor race experience.

If you are set on running the originally scheduled race, be sure to step back and understand what the time off from running means for you physiologically.

If you've taken two weeks off, adjust your race goal by 3 to 5 percent. If you've missed closer to three weeks, adjust your expected performance by 7 to 10 percent. For example, if Runner A missed two weeks of training and was shooting for a 3:30 marathon, the goal should be adjusted between 6.3 minutes (210 × 0.03) to 10.5 minutes (210 × 0.05). The new time goal would then be 3:36–3:41. If you take more than four weeks off, we suggest choosing a new race altogether.

Downtime discretion

Although we have just presented a number of ways to modify your training schedule, we contend that it is best to avoid taking unscheduled days away from training if at all possible. This applies even when your legs are tired and sore, since soreness and injury are not inextricably linked. There will be times during marathon training when your legs are achy, fatigued, and nonspecifically sore; it just comes with the territory. Many of the adaptations that happen during training occur as a result of running on the days you just don't feel like running.

If you have an injury, however, your response should be different. For less severe injuries, make sure that you are not only taking time off, but also using that time to identify the root cause of the problem. Otherwise you may continue to run into the same issue upon returning to training. For example, if you are experiencing shin splints, figure out what you need to do to reduce the pain, like getting new shoes or implementing a strength routine. If your body will allow it, reduce the volume and intensity, but continue running short and easy through the healing process. While training may need to be reduced, it doesn't necessarily have to stop completely to allow for recovery—if the cause of the injury is identified and treated, that is. When you can maintain some level of exercise, fitness losses are significantly minimized and regular training can be resumed much sooner.

The
Strategy

9

SETTING GOALS

ONCE YOU'VE CHOSEN A TRAINING PROGRAM, it's time to identify your race goals. While finding enjoyment in the day-in and day-out journey of training has its own rewards, setting a time goal for race day plays an important role in keeping you motivated. Especially on the days that you feel less than inspired, that goal can be the thing that pushes you to lace up and hit the road.

Data published in *Outside* magazine sheds some interesting light on marathon goals. Athlete-tracking platform Strava conducted a meta-analysis of 80.6 million runs logged onto their social media and training log website and app. That data, which included 1.8 million marathon runs, revealed that 70 percent of runners have a goal of finishing between 3-4 hours in the marathon. This group was running 35 miles per week, with most of their runs in the 5–10-mile range and at slower than race pace. Interestingly, the over-4-hour marathoners were running about 25 miles per week and most of their runs were shorter and faster than goal race pace.

This data illustrates that a large number of aspiring marathoners approach training in a somewhat haphazard manner. What's the point? If you're going to put all that time and effort in, why not do it the smartest and healthiest way possible, and set yourself up for the best chance of success?

Using a Race Equivalency Chart

A race equivalency chart takes your performance at one race distance, crunches numbers via some complicated algorithms, and then spits out an equal race performance at other distances.

Let's say you ran a 5K in 25:00 and want to use that as a baseline for determining your marathon goal time. As you might expect, it isn't as simple as taking the pace you ran for 3.1 miles and multiplying it. Even if you're better suited for longer distances, the rule is that as the distance increases, your pace slows. A race equivalency chart takes that slowdown into account and offers an estimated equal performance, not just an extrapolated performance. (See Table 9.1.)

Race equivalency charts help runners determine a goal with appropriate training paces. It is a very useful tool, but take care not to treat those numbers as the ultimate standard for success. Predictions made by these charts and calculators are generalized to the greater running population. They don't take into account your individual strengths and weaknesses, which renders them somewhat two-dimensional.

Let's focus on one row, highlighted below. Imagine a runner runs a 20:00 5K to establish baseline fitness. That runner then takes that 20:00 and looks across the chart to see a 3:14:58 goal marathon time.

Mile	2 mile	5K	10K	15K	10 mile	Half-mar.	25K	Marathon
5:46	12:19	20:00	41:33:00	1:04:23	1:09:37	1:32:27	1:51:17	3:14:58

The prediction assumes that our runner will be equally adept at all distances across the board. But as discussed in Chapter 4, some of us are built to be speedy at shorter distances, while others have a natural penchant for the endurance disciplines. If our runner is the former, then basing her marathon goal on a much shorter race time may only set her up for disappointment. This is particularly true because the larger the gap between the races we are comparing, the more room there is for error. That's why it is important to consider a whole constellation of factors when narrowing down your goal. The race equivalency chart offers a great jumping-off point, but is just one of the tools in your goal-setting toolbox.

TABLE 9.1 **RACE EQUIVALENCY CHART**

Mile	2 mile	5K	10K
12:59	27:43:00	45:00:00	1:33:29
12:16	26:10:00	42:30:00	1:28:17
11:32	24:38:00	40:00:00	1:23:06
11:24	24:19:00	39:30:00	1:22:03
11:15	24:01:00	39:00:00	1:21:01
11:06	23:42	38:30:00	1:19:59
10:58	23:24	38:00:00	1:18:56
10:49	23:06	37:30:00	1:17:54
10:40	22:47	37:00:00	1:16:52
10:32	22:29	36:30:00	1:15:49
10:23	22:10	36:00:00	1:14:47
10:14	21:52	35:30:00	1:13:45
10:06	21:33	35:00:00	1:12:42
9:57	21:15	34:30:00	1:11:40
9:48	20:56	34:00:00	1:10:38
9:40	20:38	33:30:00	1:09:35
9:31	20:19	33:00:00	1:08:33
9:22	20:01	32:30:00	1:07:31
9:14	19:42	32:00:00	1:06:28
9:05	19:24	31:30:00	1:05:26
8:56	19:05	31:00:00	1:04:24
8:48	18:47	30:30:00	1:03:21
8:39	18:28	30:00:00	1:02:19
8:30	18:10	29:30:00	1:01:17
8:22	17:51	29:00:00	1:00:15
8:13	17:33	28:30:00	59:12:00
8:04	17:14	28:00:00	58:10:00

15K	10 mile	Half-mar.	25K	Marathon
2:24:51	2:36:38	3:28:01	4:10:24	7:18:42
2:16:49	2:27:56	3:16:27	3:56:29	6:54:19
2:08:46	2:19:14	3:04:54	3:42:35	6:29:57
2:07:09	2:17:29	3:02:35	3:39:48	6:25:04
2:05:33	2:15:45	3:00:16	3:37:01	6:20:12
2:03:56	2:14:00	2:57:58	3:34:14	6:15:20
2:02:19	2:12:16	2:55:39	3:31:27	6:10:27
2:00:43	2:10:32	2:53:20	3:28:40	6:05:35
1:59:06	2:08:47	2:51:02	3:25:53	6:00:42
1:57:30	2:07:03	2:48:43	3:23:06	5:55:50
1:55:53	2:05:18	2:46:24	3:20:19	5:50:57
1:54:17	2:03:34	2:44:06	3:17:32	5:46:05
1:52:40	2:01:49	2:41:47	3:14:45	5:41:12
1:51:03	2:00:05	2:39:28	3:11:58	5:36:20
1:49:27	1:58:21	2:37:10	3:09:11	5:31:27
1:47:50	1:56:36	2:34:51	3:06:25	5:26:35
1:46:14	1:54:52	2:32:32	3:03:38	5:21:42
1:44:37	1:53:07	2:30:14	3:00:51	5:16:50
1:43:01	1:51:23	2:27:55	2:58:04	5:11:58
1:41:24	1:49:38	2:25:36	2:55:17	5:07:05
1:39:47	1:47:54	2:23:18	2:52:30	5:02:13
1:38:11	1:46:10	2:20:59	2:49:43	4:57:20
1:36:34	1:44:25	2:18:40	2:46:56	4:52:28
1:34:58	1:42:41	2:16:22	2:44:09	4:47:35
1:33:21	1:40:56	2:14:03	2:41:22	4:42:43
1:31:45	1:39:12	2:11:44	2:38:35	4:37:50
1:30:08	1:37:28	2:09:26	2:35:48	4:32:58

Continues

TABLE 9.1 [CONTINUED]

Mile	2 mile	5K	10K
7:56	16:56	27:30:00	57:08:00
7:47	16:37	27:00:00	56:05:00
7:39	16:19	26:30:00	55:03:00
7:30	16:00	26:00:00	54:01:00
7:21	15:42	25:30:00	52:58:00
7:13	15:24	25:00:00	51:56:00
7:04	15:05	24:30:00	50:54:00
6:55	14:47	24:00:00	49:51:00
6:47	14:28	23:30	48:49:00
6:38	14:10	23:00	47:47:00
6:29	13:51	22:30	46:44:00
6:21	13:33	22:00	45:42:00
6:12	13:14	21:30	44:40:00
6:03	12:56	21:00	43:37:00
5:55	12:37	20:30	42:35:00
5:46	12:19	20:00	41:33:00
5:37	12:00	19:30	40:30:00
5:29	11:42	19:00	39:28:00
5:20	11:23	18:30	38:26:00
5:11	11:05	18:00	37:24:00
5:03	10:46	17:30	36:21:00
4:58	10:37	17:15	35:50:00
4:54	10:28	17:00	35:19:00
4:50	10:19	16:45	34:48:00
4:45	10:09	16:30	34:17:00
4:41	10:00	16:15	33:45:00
4:37	9:51	16:00	33:14:00

15K	10 mile	Half-mar.	25K	Marathon
1:28:31	1:35:43	2:07:07	2:33:01	4:28:05
1:26:55	1:33:59	2:04:48	2:30:14	4:23:13
1:25:18	1:32:14	2:02:30	2:27:27	4:18:20
1:23:42	1:30:30	2:00:11	2:24:41	4:13:28
1:22:05	1:28:45	1:57:52	2:21:54	4:08:36
1:20:29	1:27:01	1:55:34	2:19:07	4:03:43
1:18:52	1:25:17	1:53:15	2:16:20	3:58:51
1:17:15	1:23:32	1:50:56	2:13:33	3:53:58
1:15:39	1:21:48	1:48:38	2:10:46	3:49:06
1:14:02	1:20:03	1:46:19	2:07:59	3:44:13
1:12:26	1:18:19	1:44:00	2:05:12	3:39:21
1:10:49	1:16:34	1:41:42	2:02:25	3:34:28
1:09:13	1:14:50	1:39:23	1:59:38	3:29:36
1:07:36	1:13:06	1:37:04	1:56:51	3:24:43
1:05:59	1:11:21	1:34:46	1:54:04	3:19:51
1:04:23	1:09:37	1:32:27	1:51:17	3:14:58
1:02:46	1:07:52	1:30:08	1:48:30	3:10:06
1:01:10	1:06:08	1:27:50	1:45:43	3:05:14
59:33:00	1:04:24	1:25:31	1:42:57	3:00:21
57:57:00	1:02:39	1:23:12	1:40:10	2:55:29
56:20:00	1:00:55	1:20:54	1:37:23	2:50:36
55:32:00	1:00:02	1:19:44	1:35:59	2:48:10
54:43:00	59:10:00	1:18:35	1:34:36	2:45:44
53:55:00	58:18:00	1:17:26	1:33:12	2:43:17
53:07:00	57:26:00	1:16:16	1:31:49	2:40:51
52:19:00	56:34:00	1:15:07	1:30:25	2:38:25
51:30:00	55:41:00	1:13:58	1:29:02	2:35:59

Continues

TABLE 9.1 [CONTINUED]

Mile	2 mile	5K	10K
4:32	9:42	15:45	32:43:00
4:28	9:32	15:30	32:12:00
4:24	9:23	15:15	31:41:00
4:19	9:14	15:00	31:10:00
4:15	9:05	14:45	30:38:00
4:11	8:55	14:30	30:07:00
4:06	8:46	14:15	29:36:00
4:02	8:37	14:00	29:05:00
3:58	8:28	13:45	28:34:00
3:53	8:18	13:30	28:03:00

Other Factors That Guide Goal Setting

Taking into account your individual physiology, motivations, and life circumstances is all important when deciding on a marathon goal. Before you make that final leap into training, let's consider a few other important factors.

Current and past training: Your goals should be contingent on your current foundation of training. Someone who has been injured for the past three months will need to set different goals than someone who has consistently been putting in 40-mile weeks. Some intuition is involved here. If you're the former runner who has been on the bench, err on the conservative side when setting goals. If you're the latter runner, you may not need to be quite as cautious.

Training and availability: The time you are able to lend to training has a huge influence on quality of training, and thus, the final result. When selecting a goal, take a realistic look at how much time you have to train. If you

15K	10 mile	Half-mar.	25K	Marathon
50:42:00	54:49:00	1:12:48	1:27:38	2:33:33
49:54:00	53:57:00	1:11:39	1:26:15	2:31:06
49:05:00	53:05:00	1:10:30	1:24:51	2:28:40
48:17:00	52:13:00	1:09:20	1:23:18	2:26:14
47:29:00	51:20:00	1:08:11	1:22:05	2:23:48
46:41:00	50:28:00	1:07:02	1:20:41	2:21:21
45:52:00	49:36:00	1:05:52	1:19:18	2:18:55
45:04:00	48:44:00	1:04:43	1:17:54	2:16:29
44:16:00	47:52:00	1:03:33	1:16:31	2:14:03
43:27:00	46:59:00	1:02:24	1:15:07	2:11:36

have small children or a demanding job, you might not be able to devote as much time to training as you'd like. That doesn't mean you can't train for a marathon; you just need to consider your time constraints when setting your goals. Time not only will determine how hard and long you can train on a day-to-day basis, but also how consistent you can be over a long period. In marathon training in particular, consistency makes a big difference. For example, a runner who competes well in 5Ks by logging 30–40 miles and 3–4 days per week would struggle to get in adequate training for a marathon on that same timetable. Could this runner complete a marathon running 40 miles per week? Most certainly. Would it allow for their best effort at that distance? Simply put, no.

Training window: The number of weeks and months you have to train also provides guidance in goal setting. If you're a newer runner, plan for a longer build-up period, including our 0 to 5K plan if needed. On the other hand, if, you're a veteran runner who trains consistently, the marathon-specific training block can be shorter because you already have established a good base of mileage.

External factors: Terrain, temperature, and race size can all affect your performance. If you are accustomed to training in cool and dry conditions, but your chosen race is likely to be hot and humid, adjust your final time goal to reflect that. A general rule of thumb is 5–10 seconds per mile added for every 5 degrees above 65 degrees. How much you adjust depends on your exposure to heat and humidity during training. Also, if you are going to be racing on a flat and traditionally fast course, you might predict a time slightly faster than you would on a hillier course. If you're running a very large marathon, you may want to tack a few extra minutes onto your goal time to allow for crowd management. While your chip won't start until you cross the start line, your time may still be affected by the mass of runners in front of you.

Settling on a Goal

With so many factors to take into account, how do you actually land on an appropriate time goal? At the end of the day, think of the goal-setting process as an educated guessing game. Start by looking at the race equivalency chart (Table 9.1) and plugging in a shorter distance. When you see the associated marathon time, if your reaction is "Holy smokes, there's no way!" then back off that time until you reach a time that feels challenging but realistic given your personal physiology, motivation, and life circumstances. If instead you think, "Right, let's do this!" then take into consideration the other aforementioned factors and see if you still feel that way. If you do, then go for it. You may even consider moving up the time to something slightly faster. Remember, you are always capable of a little bit more than you think. Your goal should intimidate you a bit—without scaring the heck out of you. Settle on this as your baseline goal.

As you can tell, goal setting is both a science and an art, and some instinct is involved. The truth is, your first marathon performance probably lies somewhere between what you know you can do and what terrifies you.

10

CHOOSING A RACE

WHEN I JOINED the Hansons-Brooks Distance Project in the summer of 2004, the longest race I'd ever run was a 10K. But even in college, I knew I wanted to run a marathon someday, and I had a sneaking suspicion, based on my physiology and psychology, that I would improve as the race distance increased.

Keith and Kevin offered me the opportunity to jump right into the marathon. As I began to think about my first race, I talked with them at length about training, preparation, and goals. One factor they advised me to think about before entering into serious training for a marathon was one that I had never considered: race venue. Kevin encouraged me to put myself in a position where I would have a positive experience with my first marathon. If I didn't do so, he said, I could be turned off from the event and never reach my full potential. The right race venue, he insisted, was part of that equation.

While it might sound trivial, the event you decide to run for your first marathon will play a major role in your overall experience. It can also contribute to either success or failure in terms of your goals. For instance, if you tend to panic in big crowds, running a race with 60,000 other runners might not be wise. Or if you're planning to rely on water stops along the route, you don't want to select an unsupported race that doesn't provide those amenities.

This chapter will look at factors to consider when choosing a race. Picking just the right venue can not only make for a memorable experience, but also tip the odds in your favor.

Race Venue Considerations

Just as Kevin had advised, I made a number of calculations regarding training, timing, and competition before selecting the Chicago Marathon as my first 26.2-mile race in the fall of 2004. As it happens, all that planning paid off. I loved being on the big stage in the Windy City as a 23-year-old starry-eyed kid lining up for the first race of my professional running career. The massive crowds, the flat course, and the caliber of the other runners all played into making it a great experience.

When it comes to making your own race venue selection, here are some important categories to consider.

Travel and Accommodations

My wife and I try to make a trip to the Grand Traverse Bay each year for the Bayshore Marathon. Held along the shore of Lake Michigan in Traverse City, Michigan, a town of just under 15,000 people, it can be a scramble to score a spot at the start line. The race often sells out in 15 minutes and the hotel rooms in the area are booked up soon after. Once the regular rooms are gone, your options may be limited to a pricey presidential suite or a plot of dirt at the local campsite.

This experience isn't unusual in the world of marathons. As you begin to set your sights on a particular race, a wise initial step is to make sure that you'll not only be able to get to both the city and the start line with relative ease, but that you will have a place to stay when you get there. If you are forced to find accommodations far from the start or finish, look into how you will pick up your race bib, what your options are for the pre-race dinner, and what kind of transportation you will need to secure to get to the start on race day.

Destination Distractions

If you're headed to a race in a city you've always wanted to visit, you may well be faced with quite a bit of temptation: the temptation to sightsee, the temptation to eat at that trendy or exotic restaurant you've read about, the temptation to stay out late at a club or show. There is nothing wrong with choosing a race because of the city it's in. But before race morning, resist these temptations at all costs! The last thing you want to do the day before running 26.2 miles is be on your feet all day and night, or eat a plateful of rich foods your body isn't accustomed to. If you're the type who struggles with resisting the urge to play tourist, then consider running your first marathon in a city where it's all about the race, not the destination. Or go the city of your dreams, run your race, and stay a day or two afterward, indulging in all of those temptations.

The Course

When we polled runners on social media about first marathons, one athlete quipped that he wasn't sure what he was thinking when he chose San Francisco as the site for his first race. While there are many reasons to love the Golden City, flat terrain isn't one of them. For your first marathon, your best bet is to find a race that is held on similar terrain to that which you'll train on. If you train on nothing but flat roads, then signing up for a hilly marathon adds an additional challenge to an already challenging situation. Similarly, if you log all your miles on asphalt and concrete, the gnarly terrain of a trail marathon might not play to your favor.

Take a good look at the course descriptions and elevation charts on the race website before hitting "submit" on your registration form. Many events also have course tour videos—or you can find them on YouTube. Also, don't be shy asking around. See what people from your local running group say about a race, ask other runners on social media, and read race reports on running blogs.

Time of Year

All marathon world records have been set at temperatures between 45 and 60 degrees. Not some, but all. Weather at either end of that spectrum doesn't help running performances. That's why so many marathons are held in the fall—there's a much greater chance that the temperatures will be cool—but not too cool—in most places in the US.

Temperatures that are higher or lower than the 45–60 degree range bring some challenges along with them. In higher temps, there is a greater concern for dehydration and heat-related illness, such as hyperthermia, an increase in body temp. When a runner begins to develop hyperthermia, her or she tends to show a decrease in muscular endurance. This means the muscles can't contract as forcefully for as long as they normally can. Secondly, the runner will experience a shift in metabolism. A pace that would normally feel comfortable suddenly feels much harder from an intensity standpoint. At that point, the runner starts to use carbohydrate at a much faster rate and is not able to replace it at the rate it is being used. Both of these factors result in a slower pace.

Heat also works to break down our pain tolerance and motivation, while increasing our discomfort levels and likelihood of more serious mood swings. So while 70 degrees may be perfect for a round of golf or a bike ride, it's not ideal for a marathon. Bear this in mind as you pick your race.

Another consideration is how the race date fits in with your training schedule. If you want to do a March marathon and you live in a colder part of the country, will you be able to get in quality training during the winter months? Conversely, if you live in a locale with hot summers, will you be able to train at your best in June, July, and August for a September marathon?

Race Size

Every year we receive emails from runners reporting frustration in the early miles of a race because they had to weave in and out of crowds of other runners. This scenario can lead some athletes to run faster than planned in those early miles—fueled by anger or annoyance or a desire to escape the crowd—which often sabotages the rest of their race.

In addition to interrupting the fluidity of your race performance, crowds make some of us downright claustrophobic. Bigger marathons have thousands of runners; the New York City Marathon has more than 50,000! Some runners thrive on that kind of energy. However, if you know in advance that being surrounded by hordes of other people puts you on edge, it may be best to choose a smaller race (under 2,000 runners).

Race History

Putting on a marathon is no joke; in some cases, it takes hundreds of volunteers, planning, and work hours. A race with a long history of success has been proven to have the organization and support to execute a great event. These races can usually be counted upon to have seasoned volunteers, experienced race staff, and established local backers. A brand-new race might be fantastic, but it doesn't have a track record of success to verify that. Errors such as missing water stops, uninformed volunteers, or mismarked courses can sabotage a race.

First-time races are great fun and often develop into wonderful community-building events. That said, they may not be the place to test your sea legs on your own maiden marathon voyage. Choosing a race that's well established removes a wild card and gives you one less thing to worry about.

Support

For many marathoners, encouragement, cheering, and support along the course from friends and family can make all the difference. If this is important to you, then consider choosing a marathon course that is viewer-friendly.

For example, the Chicago Marathon route is shaped like a four-leaf clover, which allows your fans to see you several times without having to move around a lot. That's a perfect situation for a first-time runner who knows that seeing a loved one is going to give him or her a boost. Other races, especially those that are point-to-point, require a lot more planning, especially if young children are among the cheerleaders.

Once you choose your race, talk things over with your friends and family and figure out what works best for your particular situation. If it's just a couple of adults who are in good health and can get around easily, this will be less of an issue. On the other hand, if you have a crowd of family and friends young and old, it might take more planning or an adjustment of expectations in terms of how many times you will get to see them on course.

Selecting the right race for your first marathon can make a real difference in the greater scheme. Travel, transportation, dinner reservations, and securing accommodations take time. Don't save these decisions for the end of training when you're already feeling under the gun. Get things ironed out early so you can slide into race day with confidence.

11

SUPPLEMENTAL TRAINING

AS YOU HAVE PROBABLY GATHERED, in order to run your best marathon, you must prepare by doing a whole lot of running. Nevertheless, there are other activities that you can do in smaller quantities to boost optimal performance and prevent injury. These include crosstraining, flexibility, and strength work. Since you want these activities to *support* your training, rather than hinder it, you have to be careful what supplemental training you include and when.

Marathon preparation is hard enough. This is not the time to begin a tae kwon do class or power-lifting regimen. That said, implementing a minimal amount of crosstraining, along with some flexibility and strength, may better your marathon performance. Not only do these types of exercises allow you to work on certain weaknesses that may be limiting your running potential, but they also provide variety to your training, making you a better overall athlete. Just remember that this is supplementing training, not replacing it.

Crosstraining

While crosstraining is a staple of some training plans, the Hansons plans limit its inclusion. The reasoning is quite simple: The most direct path to becoming a better runner is through running. This notion follows a basic principle of physiology, known as "the rule of specificity." The idea is that your body adapts specifically to the stress that it is placed under. Although a 30-minute swim is great for general fitness, it doesn't translate directly into good running performance.

If you do choose to crosstrain, be sure to consider your previous experience with a particular activity, staying away from new exercises until after the marathon. While you may be feeling fitter than ever during training, be sure to temper that zeal for exercise. You are already under considerable physical stress leading up to the marathon; adding a new activity to the mix just increases risk of injury and threatens to derail your focus. Remember: Don't start anything new until after 26.2

Runners most commonly want to add in crosstraining on their days off of running. While biking or Pilates is great for your health in almost every other circumstance, doing those activities on your off day may serve only to curb recovery from running, which makes them less productive and even potentially destructive. That said, if you always ride your bike to work and have for years, by all means, continue your routine, within reason. In this case, your body has already adapted to that exercise. If it is a long ride, however, consider taking the bus on SOS workout days. In a similar vein, if you were a Pilates junkie before marathon training, you don't need to cut your practice entirely out, but you should certainly consider cutting it down.

Be aware of the clues your body is giving you along the way. If you find you are having trouble recovering from running workouts, you shouldn't be piling on supplemental training. And if you think you may be overtraining, replacing running with a crosstraining activity isn't the answer either. If that is the case, you would benefit more from a day off so you can return to running feeling fresh the next day. If you are following the schedule and still feel you need something else beyond the recommended running, we suggest shifting your focus away from crosstraining and toward other details like flexibility and strength training. We'll discuss both in detail later in this chapter.

Some runners claim that they can't handle the higher mileage and therefore need to crosstrain to replace mileage. While this may be true for a few folks, before automatically heading to the elliptical, take a hard look at the paces you are running, the shoes you are wearing, the races you are doing, and anything else that could potentially be sabotaging your running.

If you can't seem to adapt to running mileage no matter what changes you make, you may need to step back and examine your marathon goal. If you find that you truly can't handle the mileage, then a marathon may not be your event and that's OK. Over the years, however, we have encountered far more runners who struggle to remain healthy on low-mileage/high-long-run programs than they do on the moderate weekly mileage/long-run volumes offered by the Hansons programs.

Despite our cautious approach to crosstraining, we do believe it can play a small but significant role in marathon preparation. The most obvious reason to include alternate exercises is for injury rehabilitation. If you find yourself with an injury, supplemental exercises can get you back on your feet faster by providing a reduced weight-bearing activity, allowing for increased blood flow to the injured area to promote tissue repair. Additionally, they can help maintain cardiovascular fitness, thereby making your return to running more seamless. Indeed, sitting on the couch waiting for something to heal is rarely the answer.

The key to crosstraining during injury is to find an activity that mimics running as closely as possible, such as an elliptical trainer or a stationary bike. While options like the rowing machine are great cardiovascular exercise, the emphasis is placed on the upper body and won't help the running muscles. It should be noted that the protocol can vary based on your specific injury. If you have a broken foot, for instance, biking will only aggravate the ailment further. Be cognizant of whether the activity affects the injured area and always steer clear of anything that causes pain.

Another instance in which we recommend crosstraining is during periods of planned downtime away from running. For example, after every marathon, runners in our Elite Program automatically take two weeks off from running. The 26.2 miles of pounding beats a runner up, especially after the first attempt at the distance. A two-week hiatus gives runners time to restore damaged muscles, rejuvenate the spirit, and plan the next move. Crosstraining offers the opportunity to enhance that recovery by providing a way to continue burning calories and avoid losing all of the fitness gained during marathon training.

The final reason we prescribe crosstraining is to provide a beginning runner a means through which to ease into the sport. Most first-time marathoners are taking a big step up in their weekly mileage. While ideally we would like to see everyone running 5–7 days per week, that may not be possible or even wise for some, especially at first. Adding crosstraining can contribute to the amount of aerobic fitness a person can build without doubling or tripling his or her weekly mileage over a period of a couple of months. In essence, crosstraining can bridge the gap between running three days per week and building to 5–6 days per week of running.

Flexibility and Stretching

Flexibility has long been a hot-button topic in the running community. I remember standing among my high school track team in a circle while the team captains barked out things like "hurdler stretch!" and "switch legs!" before jogging from the gym to the track to work out. For a long time, it seemed like nobody really knew what was good for us. Indeed, the term "flexibility" itself is vague. What does it mean exactly? It is simply a general label that covers a number of different ideas.

Stretching has been inextricably linked to the sport of running since the jogging craze of the 1970s, but the topic is more complex than you might think, and how you stretch can affect your running in a number of ways. By itself, flexibility refers to the maximal static (not moving) range of motion (ROM) for a particular joint. The more flexible a person is throughout his or her joint ROM, the more easily the muscles surrounding that joint can be stretched. While this makes for a more elastic muscle that is less prone to injury, it also means the muscle can't create as much power. Imagine a Stretch Armstrong doll; the more you pull his arm, the wimpier-looking he gets. In the same way, the farther you stretch a muscle, the less elastic power it will have to fire. At the end of the day, being too flexible in areas like the Achilles tendon can cause the body to be less economical because the tendon loses some of its spring-like capabilities. Being too mobile may also set you up for overuse injuries like shin splints due to weakness around the joints. On the flipside, most of us are well aware of the dangers of being inflexible. Being too tight reduces our range of motion, but also sets us up for a higher chance of overuse injuries like runner's knee and Achilles tendonitis.

While it is beyond the scope of this book to fully address flexibility, in our experience as coaches, we've found that most runners have some sort of flexibility issues. As training increases to much higher levels, a number of common ailments linked to poor flexibility tend to pop up. These can be mitigated through active stretches. When you engage in these "extra credit" exercises, you set yourself up to better handle the higher levels of training. The key is to start early into your program and make it routine.

For runners, active ROM is important. You can develop this type of flexibility through dynamic stretching, which is conducted through a set of active movements that target the running joints and muscles. To properly implement a flexibility routine, you must understand the difference between static and dynamic stretching and where they do (and do not) belong in your training. While there has been conflicting research over the years, the latest and most convincing evidence suggests that there is a time and a place for both active (dynamic) and static stretching. For both performance and injury prevention, it is important to do the right type of stretching at the right times.

Dynamic Stretching

This form of flexibility training involves rhythmic movement throughout a person's full range of motion. These motions are deliberate and controlled. One type of active stretching, often referred to as "ballistic stretching," is fast-paced, bouncy, and takes the joint beyond the natural range of motion. This can be fairly dangerous and put you at risk for injury, so we generally suggest avoiding ballistic movements. Dynamic stretching, on the other hand, focuses on proper form and motions that help to actively increase range of motion within reasonable parameters. Dynamic stretching benefits a runner in a number of ways. First and foremost, the dynamic movements reduce muscle stiffness, which decreases the risk of muscular injury. They also help prepare your body to run faster by loosening you up without stretching your muscles to the point of reducing their power. In fact, dynamic stretching can actually stimulate fast-twitch and intermediate fibers that are often neglected during traditional run training. The other advantage of this type of stretching is its influence on training the brain and the muscles to work in concert by engaging the muscle fibers and the nervous system simultaneously.

Dynamic stretching can be done before any type of run. It is effective in two key ways. First, it makes an excellent transition phase from complete rest to running. For example, because I wake up early and have a 30-minute drive to meet my team for 8 a.m. runs, I always take a few minutes before the run to do a routine similar to the one below. I feel looser and can start out a run significantly faster than I could otherwise. Second, dynamic stretching is a great way to improve running form and economy, by focusing on running-specific movements. Over time, your natural range of motion will gradually increase as well.

There are a couple of ways to implement dynamic stretching into your routine. I try to do these nearly every day due to the reasons stated above. So, for easy days, before you head out the door, simply give yourself 3–5 minutes and perform the first six exercises below. These are what we call the Dynamic Warm-Up Level 1 exercises. These are simple range-of-motion exercises and help get your body prepared for running. For an SOS day, perform the Level 1 exercise and then begin your warm-up jog of 1–3 miles. After you do your warm-up jog, perform the Level 2 exercises. These are plyometrics-based exercises and will help prepare the body to run at high intensities. Level 2 exercises are more important for speed and strength SOS days, but can certainly be done before beginning your tempo run. Level 2 exercises aren't meant to be done every day.

Dynamic Warm-Up Level 1

Arm Swings
Standing tall with feet shoulder-width apart, swing your arms in a circular, clockwise motion, mimicking propeller blades on each side of your body. Keep your back straight and knees slightly bent. After 6–10 repetitions, swing the arms from the sides across your chest in a back-and-forth motion for another 6–10 repetitions. These exercises help relax the major upper-body muscles, making your upper body more efficient during running. This is particularly advantageous because runners tend to carry tension in their arms and shoulders, which affects the rest of the stride.

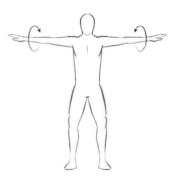

Side Bends
With the same starting posture as Arm Swings but with hands on your hips, lean smoothly from left to right, being careful not to lean backward or forward. Repeat 16–20 times. These bends assist in keeping the spine mobile.

Hip Circles

With the same posture as Side Bends, make circles with your hips, as though you are using a Hula-Hoop. Perform 10–12 rotations in a clockwise motion and then reverse direction for another 10–12 rotations. By opening up your hips, this exercise allows for a better range of motion in your stride.

Half-Squat

With the same starting posture as Hip Circles or with hands straight in front of you, bend at the knees until your thighs are parallel to the floor, then slowly straighten your legs to return to the starting position. Perform 10–12 times. The Half-Squat helps take all the major leg muscles, including the hamstrings, glutes, quads, and calves (Achilles), through their ROM.

Leg Kicks

Stand with your left side next to a wall or fence, placing your weight on your left (inside) leg and left hand on the wall/fence. Swing your right leg forward and backward in a pendulum motion for 10–12 repetitions. Reverse position and do the same with the left leg.

Leg Swings

Stand facing the wall/fence with both hands on the wall/fence, placing your weight on your left leg. Swing your right leg across the front of your body. Swing it as far left as you can move comfortably and then back to the right as far as you can move comfortably. Do 10–12 times and switch legs.

Dynamic Warm-Up Level 2

Slow Skipping
Skip slowly for 30–50 meters (10–15 seconds.)
Turn around and skip back to your starting point.

High Knees
Jog slowly and focus on lifting your knees toward your chest in a marching fashion. Pay attention to driving the knee toward the chest, and also maintain proper arm carriage and pump rhythmically with the opposite knee. (Proper arm carriage means elbows bent 90 degrees and moving back and forth as if on a pendulum at the shoulder.) The up-and-down actions should be quick, but your movement forward should be steady and controlled. Travel 30–50 meters, then return to start.

Butt Kicks
In this reverse motion of High Knees, pull your heels back rapidly toward your rear end. Again, the motions should be quick, but your linear movement steady. Travel 30–50 meters, turn, and continue back to your starting position.

Cariocas
Also known as the grapevine, this is the trickiest of the exercises in terms of coordination. With arms perpendicular to your torso or bent at your sides, stand with feet shoulder-width apart. Moving to the left, pull your right foot behind the left. Sidestep to the left, then cross the right leg in front of the left. Continue with this motion. Basically, the legs are twisting around each other while the torso stays still on the twisting pelvis. Travel 30–50 meters, turn, and continue these steps back to your starting position.

Bounders

These are a similar motion to High Knees, except instead of driving the knees high into the chest, focus on pushing off with your trailing leg and driving forward. It is a cross between Slow Skipping and High Knees. Travel 30–50 meters, turn, and continue back to your starting position.

Sprints

To close out the routine, do 4–6 repetitions of a 75–100-meter sprint at near-maximal effort. Always do your fast running with the wind, so jog back against the wind to start a new sprint. The sprints shouldn't last more than 15 seconds, so slower runners should begin with 75-meter sprints.

By actively engaging the muscles and getting the neuromuscular connections firing, you are (1) preparing your body to run fast, (2) working on specific running motions that will aid in proper form development, and (3) developing a neuromuscular connection to fast and intermediate muscle fibers that will serve as a major advantage late in the marathon when your slow-twitch fibers are fried. If you are looking to improve performance without sacrificing a lot of time, then we strongly suggest adding a dynamic routine to your training toolbox.

Static Stretching

When most people talk about stretching, they are referring to static flexibility. Unlike dynamic stretching, static stretching is done standing or sitting still, rather than using an active motion. For years, runners have performed static stretching routines before workouts and races. Ironically, this is probably the worst time for this type of movement as it reduces your muscles' ability to produce force because it stretches the muscles too much. The muscles lose their elasticity as they are stretched, making them less powerful and also putting you at risk for a muscle tear. Even so, there is a place for static stretching in your training toolbox; you just have to know when and how to use it.

When is the best time for static stretching? The answer depends on what you hope to achieve from the stretch. There has been much research to support the use of static stretching after a workout as a means of injury prevention. For instance, calf tightness has been shown to be associated with pronation of the rear foot, which causes the tibia and fibula (lower leg bones) to internally rotate, a pain that is commonly referred to as shin splints. More specifically, this kind of inflexibility can lead to tendonitis, stress fractures, Achilles tendon injuries, and knee issues. Poor flexibility also tends to cause the front of the pelvis to tilt forward, creating excessive curvature in the lower back. The result of all this is a tightening of the lower back muscles, which predisposes the runner to back injuries. However, we have to be careful of what our definition of "after a workout" means. Immediately following an easy run, doing the following light static stretching routine (LS) is fine. It promotes muscle health and helps you feel better. But if you are trying to improve your tissue length, then save the static stretching for several hours after an intense workout.

Light Static Stretching Postworkout

The following nine stretches should be performed post-run, holding for 20 seconds; perform 1–3 repetitions each. Do not stretch to the point of pain or until the muscle shakes; rather, keep each movement slow and controlled. These stretches should be incorporated into your daily routine, and the whole sequence will take about 10–15 minutes. If you are in a rush, the routine can be done later in the day, but not prior to a run.

WHERE DOES STRETCHING FIT INTO MY TRAINING PLAN?

Stretching that is movement-based, such as dynamic warm-ups, drills, and sprints, should be done prior to your main run. For example, doing Dynamic Warm-Up 1 before your runs will get your muscles prepped for the coming exercise. Save Dynamic Warm-Up 2 for SOS days (except long runs). These should be performed after your jogging warm-up but before the workout. They are designed to prepare the body for fast running. Static stretching should be saved for after easy runs. This type of stretching can also be done after your cooldown following SOS workouts. There is an exception: Static stretching used to increase muscle length should be saved for either a few hours before or after runs—treat this type of stretching more like a stand-alone exercise or workout.

Low Back

Lie flat on your back. Draw both legs toward your chest. For a stretch, place hands behind knees and pull knees close to chest. This stretch will isolate the long back muscles running from the pelvis to the shoulder blades.

Shoulder

Stand upright with feet shoulder-width apart. Extend your right arm in front of you so that it is perpendicular to the torso. Place your left hand on your right elbow or slightly above it, then gently pull the right arm across your chest toward your left side. Repeat with the left arm. We tend to carry tension in our shoulders. Many runners pull their shoulders up when they get tired, creating poor form and wasting energy. This move reduces that effect.

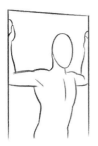

Chest

Stand upright facing an open doorway, feet shoulder-width apart. One foot should be slightly in front of the other for balance. With your arms extended straight out to the sides (you should look like a T), place your arms against the wall on either side of the doorway, palms touching the wall. Lean forward until you feel a gentle stretch in the pectoral muscles and biceps. Many runners tend to have very tight chest muscles that cause them to hunch their upper back. This stretch fights poor posture and form that can lead to inefficient running.

Calves

Stand a foot or two away from a wall, leaning forward so your hands are bracing you against the wall. Keeping the right foot stationary, slide the left foot back another 12 inches. Your heels should stay on the floor. As your chest gets closer to the wall, slightly bend the right leg to stretch the calf muscle. Repeat for the left leg. Added flexibility in the calf muscles helps you to avoid potential pronation and tendon problems.

Gluteal

Lie on your back on a soft, flat surface. Bend your right leg so that the knee is pointing upward but the foot is still flat on the floor. Next, fold your left leg so that the ankle of that leg is resting on your right knee. Your left leg should be perpendicular to your right leg. Interlock your hands within the fold of the right leg, pulling the right knee toward your chest as far as you comfortably can. Repeat on the opposite side.

Groin

Stand upright with your feet wider than shoulder-width apart. As you squat, extend your left leg to the side, so your right leg is squatting. If needed for balance, place your hands on your right knee. You should feel a stretch along the inside of the left leg. Switch sides and repeat.

Hamstrings

Sit on a flat, soft surface. Bend the right knee so that the bottom of the right foot is touching the inside of the left thigh and the right leg rests on the floor. The left leg should be straight out from the body with a slight bend at the knee. Slowly bend from the waist so that the stretch is truly focused on the hamstring muscle group and not the upper back. Repeat with the left leg.

Hip Flexors/Quads

Step forward with your right leg as if performing a lunge; your left leg should be extended behind you, left knee touching the floor. Your right knee should be directly above your right ankle. Keeping the torso straight, push your hips forward so that your right knee is past your right ankle and your left knee is behind your hips. You should feel the stretch in your left hip flexors and quadriceps. Repeat on the other side.

Hips

Sit on the floor with your left leg extended, right leg crossed over left. Your right foot will be on the outside of your left leg. Next, place your left arm so that the elbow is on the outside (left side) of the right knee. Your right arm should be a brace near the hip. Twist to the right by using your left arm as a lever against the right leg. Repeat on the opposite side.

The purpose behind stretches 5–9 is identical. The muscles in the pelvis are used for stability, but they can also limit range of motion. If these muscles are tight, the natural stride length is diminished, leading to a decrease in running economy. By keeping these muscles flexible and allowing free range of motion, you maximize your natural stride length.

If your goal is to actually lengthen the tissue, then these stretches should be held for a longer period, which does involve some discomfort. When we are lengthening the tissues, we are basically pulling apart a knotted mess of muscle fibers. While increasing tissue length is uncomfortable, the good news is that you do not do this type of stretching for all muscles. Most people need this only for their Achilles, hip flexors, and maybe hamstrings.

Hold these stretches for 3–5 minutes, to a point of slight discomfort. Remember, change takes time; even if you do these every day, it will be about 12 weeks before you see noticeable improvement. When you begin, you may find 3–5 minutes to be difficult to hold, so don't worry if you can begin with only 1–2 minutes at the beginning. If that's the case, try and add a minute every 1–2 weeks until you can get into that 3–5 minute hold.

Where does yoga fit in? Yoga may be a great alternative to going through a traditional flexibility routine. Since it is more like a static stretch, the same rules would apply by going through a routine either several hours before or after an SOS day. It would be fine to go straight from an easy run to a yoga routine. Doing gentle yoga on an off day is perfectly acceptable as well.

Strength Training

Some runners also supplement their workouts with strength (resistance) training. Increased strength contributes to better running in a number of ways. First and foremost, it helps to improve form, especially as you become fatigued. Recently we did a VO_2max test on an athlete, watching her form as she progressed through the test. During the latter stages, her posture notably deteriorated, especially in her lower back. This caused her shoulders to round and her stride to shorten significantly. In a follow-up test 14 weeks later, she performed the same test; however, in the interim she followed our basic training plan and incorporated some of the strength training discussed below. The results were amazing. Not only was she able to go about 6 minutes longer on the test, but she also maintained good form throughout. Two weeks later, she set a personal record (PR) at her marathon by more than 8 minutes.

In addition to improved performance, strength training can also assist in preventing injuries through the protective effects of stronger muscles.

What's more, it helps you fight fatigue by training the body to be able to draw from fast-twitch fibers late in an endurance event.

A number of different exercises belong under the strength-training umbrella, including the dynamic drills described in the previous section, core-muscle training, and free weights.

Some runners avoid strength training, worried about putting on bulk and gaining weight. While the theory is correct, in reality it is fairly difficult to add any significant muscle mass onto your body weight. If the right exercises are done in the correct volumes, the average runner won't have to worry about putting on extra pounds. In other words, spending 30 minutes 2–3 days per week doing basic strength training is not going to turn you into a linebacker. Just a stronger, better runner.

There are many options for adding strength training to your running program. Our basic philosophy involves three main ideas:

1.   It should complement the running regimen; strength work should never replace running.

2.   It should improve weaknesses, muscle imbalances, and running form; in essence, strength training should help to improve running performance.

3.   It should be short and simple.

Within strength training, there are levels. Just as we wouldn't throw brand-new runners into an interval workout their first day, we would not ask someone new to strength training to do Olympic lifts right out of the gate. Rather, we start with basic bodyweight and movement exercises. If you incorporate the dynamic stretching component along with the routine below, then you are well on your way to becoming stronger. Start with these two com-

WHERE DOES STRENGTH TRAINING FIT INTO MY TRAINING PLAN?

There are two theories about when it's best to incorporate strength training into your marathon program. The first theory is to do everything on a hard day. So, if you did a speed workout in the morning, you would do your strength training that evening. In this way, you keep your easy days completely easy. The second theory is exactly the opposite: Do your strength training on your easy days. Most of the reasoning behind this second theory is ease of timing. If you are running a short, easy day, you can then go right from that into a core routine or similar for 15 minutes and then go on with your day.

As for which theory to choose, it's fine to do what fits your schedule best. However, there is one exception: Allow at least a few hours between an SOS workout and any heavy weight lifting. If you are lifting on an easy day, it is fine to go right from your run to lifting if you choose.

ponents for several weeks. Once you feel you have mastered these, you can consider adding resistance strength training.

The routine should not take more than 10 minutes to complete, and implementation is pretty flexible. If you run in the morning, you can do these right after an easy run or wait and do them during a break at work or in the evening as you watch TV. If you run at night, follow the same logic, doing strength training right after an easy run, or waiting until the next morning, perhaps while your coffee brews!

Strength: Body-Weight and Movement Exercises

Back Extension

Lie facedown on the floor, with the majority of your weight on your stomach. Extend both legs with feet about shoulder-width apart, and extend both arms straight out in front of you. (Alternately, rest your hands on the small of your back.) Contract the lower back muscles and square off your shoulders so that your entire back is straightened. Hold for 2–3 seconds and release. Repeat 12–15 times. During running, the back absorbs a lot of force upon each footstrike; the stronger it is, the better it will handle this shock. Variation: This may also be done on an exercise ball, with your body balanced on the ball at your hips and your toes on the floor for balance.

Superman

The Superman is similar to the Back Extension, but instead of simply contracting the back muscles in a stationary position, you lift one arm and the opposite leg. Lying facedown, lift your left arm and right leg at the same time. This strengthens the arms, glutes, and back in one shot. Hold each contraction for 1–2 seconds before releasing. Repeat 12–15 times on each side. Having a strong upper back means less shoulder slouching and promotes proper posture and upper-body running motion. Variation: This may also be done on an exercise ball.

Squat

Stand with feet shoulder-width apart, hands at your sides. Flex your hips and knees as if sitting in a chair. Aim to get your rear end as close to the floor as you are able, in a deep squat, in order to engage glutes and hamstrings. If you can't go past a 90-degree angle in your hips, then go as far as you can. Over time, as you continue practicing, you will be able to deepen your squat. Start with 10-15, and build to 20 over the course of several weeks.

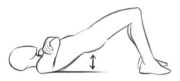

Bridge

Lie on your back on the floor with both legs bent and feet flat on the floor. Ideally your arms will be crossed over your chest, but you can extend them to the side if needed for stability. Rise up by contracting the glutes, back, and hamstring muscles. Keep your back straight, neither dipping your hips not arching your back. The only points of contact with the floor should be the shoulders and the feet. Hold each contraction for 1–3 seconds and perform 12–15 repetitions. As this becomes easier, you can move to a one-legged version, with one leg bent and the other leg straight and raised off the floor. Remember to change legs as you repeat. This is intended to strengthen the glutes and hamstrings, which are often weaker than the quads due to running. It also stretches the notoriously tight hip flexors.

Side Plank

While the traditional plank focuses on the front abdominals, the side plank focuses on the obliques, or side abdominals. Lie on your right side. Then bend your right arm so that the humerus bone, or the bone between the shoulder and elbow, is the "post" and your forearm is on the floor, perpendicular to the rest of

your body. Your right foot should rest on the floor with your left foot on top of it. Don't sag in the midsection or bend at the waist. Hold the position for 10–20 seconds, then repeat on the left side. Increase the duration as you get stronger. This exercise helps to balance strength between the front and side abdominal muscles.

Plank

Place your forearms on the floor with elbows aligned below your shoulders, and arms parallel to the body about shoulder-width apart. Raise your legs and torso off the floor so your weight is on your forearms and toes. You want to create a straight line from ankles to head. Prevent your rear end from sticking up or drooping down. These should be done until failure. At first, you may only be able to hold for 30 seconds. After you can hold good form for 1–2 minutes, feel free to add more sets or seek out variations to the basic plank.

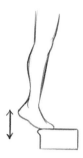

Eccentric Calf Raise

Using a step or a curb, stand on tiptoes with your heel extending past the edge of the raised surface. Allow your heel to drop below curb level by a couple inches—your heel will be lower than your toes. Rise back to starting position. You can rest your arms at your sides or hold onto a railing for balance. Start with at least one set of 15–20 repetitions and build to 2–3 sets of repetitions.

These strength exercises offer an all-encompassing introduction to resistance training. Consider adding them to your running regimen and you'll notice a difference in a matter of weeks. While running can take up much of your time, strength training is a quick and easy way to potentially boost performance and ward off injuries.

Once you have adapted to the bodyweight and movement exercises, consider upping your game by adding weight. Weight can be in the form of dumbbells, tubes or bands, medicine balls, machines, or free weights. Use what you are comfortable with. No matter which you choose, your muscles will get stronger.

Strength: Resistance Training

These exercises should be done in 1–3 sets of 10–12 reps. You may need to start with one set and add another as you feel stronger. At the end of the last few reps, you should be at the point of fatigue—you'll feel like you can't do another rep with proper form. This is important, as it is these last, fatigued reps that promote the greatest adaptations.

Use a weight that feels heavy to you, but not so heavy that you can't do at least 10 reps. Essentially, you want to be fatigued to the point where you can't hold proper form by roughly the 12th repetition. However, it is going to this "failure" that is the most important, so whether it is 10 or 15 reps, that's fine. Remember all movements should be controlled, and recovery should be about 60 seconds between each set.

Upper Body

Chest Press

Lie on your back on a bench or floor, arms extended to sides with dumbbell in each hand, elbows bent at 90 degrees. Bend legs so that feet are flat on the floor. Push dumbbells up and away from your chest so that arms are extended and perpendicular to your body. Lower in the same manner until weights are slightly below shoulder line or until arms contact the floor.

Shoulder Press

Sit on a bench or chair with back support, with feet flat on the floor. Hold dumbbells with arms raised and elbows bent at a 90-degree angle. Weights should be about ear height on either side. Press weights up until arms are extended; be careful not to lean so far back that you feel the chair back. Lower weights back to starting position.

Kneeling Row

Holding a weight in your right hand, stand so your left side is next to a bench. Place your left hand and left knee on the bench so that your back is parallel to the bench. With right arm extended toward the floor, pull weight toward chest until weight is at chest level. Slowly extend arm back to starting position. Perform all reps on one side before doing the opposite side.

Lower Body

Dumbbell Deadlift

Stand with feet shoulder-width apart, a dumbbell to the outside of each foot. Squat and pick up dumbbells (one in each hand). Torso should be bent at waist, roughly parallel to the floor. Lift by extending legs first and then your back. Gently lower your back, then your legs, to starting position.

Dumbbell Squat

Holding a dumbbell in each hand, stand with feet shoulder-width apart and toes pointing straight forward. Arms should be straight, close to your sides, palms facing your body. Lower by pushing hips back and bending knees. Lower yourself as far as range of motion allows while keeping legs parallel to each other and back straight. Return slowly back to starting position.

Side Lunges

Stand with feet shoulder-width apart, holding a dumbbell centered at chest height and close to body. Knees should be slightly bent. With left leg anchored, step wide to the left so that the left knee is bent at a 90-degree angle. Your right leg should stay straight. Step back up by extending the left leg and returning to the starting position. Alternate sides until you have completed 12 lunges for each side.

12

RECOVERY

WHEN RUNNERS WANT TO SHOW EVIDENCE of improved running performance, they generally reference hard numbers related to pace and mileage. In my own running life, I have been asked more times than I can count, "What was your mileage last week?" But I don't think I've ever been asked, "How much recovery did you get in last week?" That's because many of us overlook the importance of strategically placed R&R. Indeed, some dismiss that time as a "waste." But here's the truth: We can talk all we want about crushing workouts and getting in monster miles, but none of that matters if we don't recover from those efforts.

At Hansons, we talk a lot about cumulative fatigue, so you may wonder how rest and recovery fit into that picture. This chapter will help you understand the different kinds of fatigue, and how to aim for cumulative fatigue without tipping over into overcooking.

Fatigue: Acute vs. Cumulative vs. Overtraining

When training for a marathon, it's common to experience some tiredness and fatigue. In fact, it's a normal part of the process and welcome to a point. After all, you're asking a lot of your body. That said, there are different levels of fatigue, and being aware of the symptoms and signs of each is important.

Acute fatigue: You feel this after doing a single bout of work. If you are a new runner, you may feel this after every run for the first few weeks, as your body works to adapt to the new stress it is being subjected to. On the other hand, seasoned runners may feel this only after SOS days, and in particular, those types of workouts that don't suit their strengths. For instance, if you struggle with long runs but can zip through speed days without any trouble, which one do you expect you will have the hardest time recovering from? Correct: the long run. The same is true for anything that doesn't fit your running strengths.

This state is called "acute fatigue" because it is relatively short-lived. If you approach your recovery with the same diligence that you do your training, then within 48 hours, the fatigue you feel from that workout should be negligible.

Acute fatigue is crucial to development. The body responds to the stress you put on it by entering into a state of alarm. A hard workout can throw your body off its baseline, and since the body wants to be in homeostasis, it releases stress hormones in order to adapt to the stress you just put it under. The next time the body experiences that stress, it is better equipped to handle it. That's what training adaptations—and alarming the body and putting it in state of eustress (the good kind of stress)—is all about.

When it comes to proper recovery from acute fatigue, keep two things in mind. One, although it takes 24–48 hours to recover from a hard session, this does not mean you take the next 1–2 days off, unless indicated on your plan. While you certainly don't want to complete another hard SOS workout the following morning, you can and should crosstrain or go for an easy run. In the schedules, you will see that most of the off days prescribed are labeled as "off or crosstrain." We call this "relative recovery," because it is recovery relative to what you did the day before. In this time frame, you can still replenish glycogen stores, rehydrate, and repair tissue. At this point, the body is in its super compensation phase—overcompensating for the hard workout you did the previous day.

When, then, is your body ready for the next SOS day? Depending on the person and the workout, the next SOS should be 36–72 hours later. If you wait any longer than that, your body will begin to head back to its previous baseline. If you wait less than 36 hours, you risk your body leaving that desirable state of eustress and going into distress (the bad kind of stress), which can lead to injury, illness, and overtraining. We've strategically placed SOS days throughout the training plans to address this and take the guesswork out of it for you.

Cumulative fatigue: One of the major tenets of the Hansons program is the fatigue you accrue over time and training. As just discussed, each time we stress our body, we cause acute fatigue. How fast we recover from that fatigue depends on factors we will address later in this chapter, such as nutrition, hydration, and sleep. It also depends on the amount of stress you placed on the body—an easy day is far less stressful than an SOS day.

As your marathon training proceeds, chances are, you won't be 100 percent recovered from week to week. And that's a good thing. The goal is actually to keep your body in that state of low-level fatigue—eustress—during the compensation phase of training. This part of your training—the last 8–10 weeks of the schedules—is when we are doing the most work that is specific to your race. It will be the time where the SOS work is primarily strength, 8–10-mile tempos, and the longest long runs. As you approach that main part of your training, you will enter a phase of functional overreaching, or cumulative fatigue. During this phase, you will find training feels harder. You will be sore, you will want to eat everything you see, and you will be tired. However, you should still be able to successfully complete your workouts. The plans are designed to keep you in this state of cumulative fatigue for the last six weeks before you begin the taper. Your taper then allows all of the super-compensation—physiological adaptations—to take place as you recover. Following this bit of recovery time, you will be at the highest level of your personal potential for race performance.

Overtraining: This is when you've gone a step too far. Our plans are designed to help you peak for your race, rather than push to the point of diminishing returns. The differentiating factor between being in a state of cumulative fatigue and being overtrained is performance. Say you feel sluggish and fatigued heading into your Thursday tempo run. If you are in a state of cumulative fatigue, you may not feel great, but you'll still come close to hitting your prescribed pace. Even as it gets hard, you'll still be able to find that extra gear and grind it out over the last couple miles. If you are overtrained, however, you will not be able to do that. Not even close. You might not even be able to finish the workout at all. That said, we all have bad days, so don't immediately draw conclusions or shut things down after a bad workout or even a few lackluster sessions. However, if your workouts and general state of well-being continue to feel as though they are trending in the wrong direction, then it may be time to evaluate your current state of fitness, as well as potentially your marathon goal time.

Balancing Act

The balance between adapting to training and blunting the training response can be a fine line. We will discuss ways to combat soreness and promote quick recovery, while still promoting adaptation. There are a lot of "extras" you can do with recovery, as well as many hocus-pocus products that promise to speed your recovery. But Hansons has two rules of thumb when it comes to recovery: Master the basics and keep it simple. So here we'll put the focus on the basic things you can do to ensure that your recovery is as solid as your training.

ADJUSTING TRAINING TO FIT YOUR NEEDS

Chapter 2 posed questions that encouraged you to consider your individual traits as a runner. One of those asked you to think about how well you recover from training workouts. Why is it important to know this? Because you can then adapt your training program to accommodate your needs. While Hansons plans are highly structured, they are not rigid, and there's nothing in the rules that says you can't move days around. For instance, if you find it hard to do a long run on Sunday and then turn around and do another hard effort on Tuesday, then you might consider doing your long run on Saturday instead and moving Saturday's run to Sunday. That will give you an extra full day to recover from the long run. For more on modifying your schedule, see Chapter 8.

Active Recovery

While active recovery can mean many things, for our purposes here, it refers to the cooldown on your SOS days, as well as the easy days, especially the day after an SOS day. The cooldown should be looked at as the opposite of a warm-up. In a warm-up, you are prepping the body to run fast. Your cooldown is to prep the body to go back to a resting state. Although runners are often crunched for time, know that getting in even a 1-mile or 10-minute jog following a hard workout can be a big help to your overall recovery.

Your easy days, especially after an SOS day, are also crucial to your recovery. Unfortunately, this is where many runners get overzealous, especially early on in training. They feel good after harder workouts, and as a result, run their easy days too fast. Be sure to slow these runs down to a light intensity; if you are breathing too hard to carry on a conversation, then you are running too fast. In the plans in this book, the day following an SOS workout is either a rest day or an easy run of around 40 minutes (maybe a little longer depending on pace).

204 | HANSONS FIRST MARATHON

What you will find is that over time, you will feel less sluggish and lethargic following a workout. This in turn allows more consistent days running, continual aerobic stimulus/adaptation, and quicker improvements in performance.

If your schedule indicates an off day following an SOS day, that is not a free ticket to do nothing at all. An off day is a perfect time to engage in a simple walk, a strength training session, yoga, or a bike ride at a light intensity. The key is to make it a light session that doesn't go beyond 60 minutes.

Recovery Off the Trails

When it comes to recovery, the things you choose to do when you *aren't* running or crosstraining offer the biggest payoffs. In the same way you don't expect your car to run without periodic oil changes, gas in the tank, and the occasional tire rotation, you can't expect your body to perform at its best if you aren't tending to the basics. These include sleep, nutrition, stretching, ice baths, compression gear, and massage.

Sleep

Despite its utmost importance, quality sleep is something that eludes many. A good night's rest offers two major benefits. One, protein synthesis (the making of protein) occurs at a high level overnight. Letting that happen allows muscles to repair faster. Two, during a deep phase of sleep called Rapid Eye Movement (REM), growth hormone is released. This anabolic compound triggers adaptation in exercised muscles while promoting growth even during recovery.

How much sleep do you need? According to Sage Rountree's *The Athlete's Guide to Recovery,* 8 hours of sleep per night should be your baseline. After that, we need more based on how much training we do. For 10 hours of training in a week, add an extra hour per day (9 hours). For 15 hours of training, aim for 9.5 hours a night, and for 20 hours of training per week, 10 hours a night. These time frames are ideal for optimal recovery, but we understand that life intervenes, and you'll often get less than the ideal amount. If the recommended volume of sleep is not going to be attainable, do everything you can to maximize the sleep that you can get. Here are some tips to help you reach REM sleep quicker.

> Make sure your room is cool, dark, and quiet

> Create a good routine (in bed at same time, up at same time)

> Avoid watching TV in bed (or smartphone/tablet screens)

> Don't consume caffeine 4–5 hours before bed

> Be careful of fluid consumption prior to sleep

> Eat a higher carbohydrate meal up to 3 hours before bed

> Take in 20 grams of high-quality (preferably whey) protein before bed

> Try a magnesium-based sleep spray or quality supplement

Naps are also beneficial. Rountree suggests that naps should either be a quick powernap of 20 minutes or one of more than 90 minutes—not in between. Ideally, if you can sneak a longer nap in every so often, do it! That's when growth hormone is released to spur recovery and adaptation. She suggests avoiding naps in the 45-minute range, as many times afterthat amount of sleep we wake up groggy so it's tougher to return to work or workouts.

Refueling and rehydrating

Nutrition also offers a high return on investment. Simply eating a balanced diet and hydrating will help speed your recovery along. We discuss nutrition and hydration in detail in Chapter 13, but in this section, we will focus on basic fuel and fluid for immediate recovery following workouts.

Refueling after a workout is crucial. Our bodies have an extremely limited stored amount of carbohydrate, and the longer and more intense a workout is, the more depleted you become. Your goal is to ingest 1.2 grams of carbo-hydrates per kilogram of bodyweight as soon as possible after that workout. For a 150-pound person, this is about 82 grams and might include a sports bar and fluids or chocolate milk and a banana. This gets the recovery process moving right away. Consume this same amount of carbohydrate a couple more times over the next two hours.

On SOS days, you should aim to ingest 5–7 grams of carbohydrates per kilogram of bodyweight after the workout. For most of my athletes, that is 300–400 grams of carbohydrate during the day. That may sound like a lot, but when you are training at high intensities for longer periods of time, you deplete your glycogen stores. That said, if you are fueling during your workout, that certainly cuts into what you will need throughout the rest of the day. As for protein, you should get in at least 20 grams of high-quality protein as soon as possible after an SOS workout, and 20–40 would be even better. You should also be aiming for 20 grams of protein at every meal during the day and before bed. This will help you hold on to that precious lean muscle tissue and ensure that any weight you do lose is fat weight.

Rehydrating is as important as refueling. Within five hours of completing a tough workout or on a hot day, try to replace about 150 percent of the fluid you've lost. To do this precisely, you can weigh yourself immediately before and after your run to determine how much water you sweated out. If you lose two pounds on the run, take in three pounds of fluid within the next five hours. To maximize your rehydration strategy, space out this intake. If you attempt to drink the total amount immediately after your workout, you'll urinate out what the intestine cannot absorb. Breaking the intake into two or three rounds will result in more of that fluid staying in your body. Also, ensure you have sodium in some of the fluid you're taking in, such as in a sports drink. This will help your body better retain the fluid rather than urinating the excess out. This will also assist you in gauging how much fluid you will need to replace during the race itself. We'll talk about that in more detail in Chapter 13.

Stretching/Flexibility

Stretching has its place in recovery; however, as discussed in Chapter 11, it is not immediately after your workout. Focus instead on hydration and refueling in the short window of time after your workout and save stretching for several hours before or after the workout. If you just can't break that habit of stretching postworkout, be sure to keep it very light, and as soon as you feel the slightest discomfort, back off. A light mobility routine after a run or workout is probably a better choice than a static stretching routine.

Ice Baths

Ice baths promote vasoconstriction. This "closing off" of the arteries prevents blood from entering injured tissue. The short-term effect is a reduced amount of inflammation and pain. While this may sound desirable, our bodies actually need inflammation to heal tissue. We also need inflammation to promote long-term adaption. If we block that inflammation, there's nothing telling our body that it needs to adapt to the stress it has been placed under because the markers that trigger adaptation are being blocked. So save the ice baths for a special treat. Perhaps after a weekend long run, do a cold soak as a way of resetting for your upcoming week. Just do not get in the habit of doing them several times per week. Here are other tips to make your ice bath effective.

> ❭ Soak for 10–15 minutes after a 2-plus-hour long run or an intense 90-minute SOS

> ❭ Use 50–55 degree water

> ❭ Perform within 60 minutes of your run (within 15 minutes is best)

Compression Gear

The jury is still out as to whether compression gear truly aids in recovery or performance. Regardless, many runners swear by it and we think there is a place for it, especially when it comes to practical items such as compression socks. In an ideal world, you'd get off your feet and relax after a hard workout, but most of us don't have that kind of time. Wearing a pair of compression socks can certainly help you feel better, if nothing else. If you choose to wear compression socks, we recommend that you wear them for twice as long as your workout. So if you did a 2-hour run, then wear the socks for about four hours. This is true especially if you are going straight from a workout to a situation in which you'll be on your feet for a significant amount of time.

Massage

Massage releases the tension of worked muscles and helps manage inflammation. A longer-term approach to massage includes breaking down scar tissue and muscle adhesions. One session won't change the structure of your muscles, but if you have the time and can afford it, a good deep-tissue massage every few weeks is excellent. If not, try to get one once a month during your marathon training. If you make massage a regular part of your routine, you'll find that your muscles are more resilient, you'll bounce back from workouts quicker, and you'll have fewer aches and pains. Your last deep tissue massage should be about three weeks out from your race.

Recovery from the training we do is as vital as the training we are trying to recover from. There are many options out there and fortunately for us, the simplest ones (sleeping, rehydrating, and refueling) offer us the biggest return on investment. When you start to reach that point of uncertainty between training hard and overtraining, take stock of what your recovery has been like. You may just need to make a few small tweaks to keep the training at a high level.

Next, we'll delve deeper into the topic of nutrition and hydration, which have equally influential ramifications when it comes to running performance.

WHAT TYPE OF MASSAGE IS BEST FOR RUNNERS?

As a runner, it is generally best to see someone who works with athletes and has experience specifically in sports massage. Keep in mind that there are many techniques out there and what works for one person might be less effective for another. As an elite competitive athlete, I find great benefit in seeing a massage therapist who focuses on deep tissue work and is certified in Rolfing. This technique involves manipulating the tendons and fascia of the muscle. I regularly get this type of bodywork done every two weeks during training and then go for a lighter and gentle massage about 1–2 weeks out from a major competition.

13

NUTRITION AND HYDRATION

SMART FUELING AND HYDRATION will play crucial roles in your marathon success. You may have heard the saying, "You can't out-train a poor diet," and as a coach and an athlete, I assure you this is true. Furthermore, the more you try to train, the more a poor diet is exposed. Never underestimate the fundamental importance of fuel and hydration choices. Simple tweaks to your nutrition can vastly improve both your health and performance. Although important for all runners, this is particularly important when training for long distance races like the marathon. While good nutrition can certainly play a role in your success in a 5K or 10K, it becomes increasingly vital as you add mileage and intensity. We are not registered dietitians, so our advice here comes directly from years of coaching and competing. While we provide general recommendations, be sure to seek medical advice or consult a sports nutritionist for more specific guidelines.

Marathon Nutrition

Hard training requires that you consider three important aspects of nutrition: consuming enough calories, consuming the right calories, and consuming calories at the right times. Once you have these things dialed in, you will be well on your way to building an optimal base of fuel for training and racing.

Consuming Enough Calories

The first step to taking control of your nutrition and diet is knowing how many calories you will need throughout the day. Marathon training is a major undertaking and your caloric needs will be different than they are during periods of inactivity, casual exercise, or training for shorter races. They will also vary from day to day. By taking in the right amount of calories, you'll maintain a healthy weight and support your training. Large calorie deficits can sabotage your training and performance, leading to issues with overtraining, illness, and injury. The runners who are afraid of eating too much tend to also be the ones who end up getting burned out or injured— oftentimes as early as 6 weeks into hard training. If you find yourself in this camp, examine your calorie consumption first. When an athlete reports fatigue, sluggishness, and difficulties with training (and life), the first thing we look at is training paces, and a close second is caloric intake. Sometimes athletes can get away with consistent caloric deficits early on because the training is low and they have gone through it before. However, as the training increases, needs increase and they find themselves beginning to struggle. Why? Because they are running on fumes.

Calculating caloric needs

Some basic formulas can be utilized to give you an idea of how many calories you need on a daily basis. They are pretty simple to use and accurate enough to give you a general range indicating what is appropriate for you based on body weight and level of exercise.

To convert pounds to kilograms (kg), take weight in pounds and divide by 2.2.
To convert inches to centimeters (cm) take height in inches and multiply by 2.54

Your caloric needs are based on three basic components. The first is your Resting Metabolic Rate (RMR). This is the bare minimum of calories you need to keep your brain and organs functioning. The second is your Daily Activity Expenditure (DAE). This is the number of calories you burn throughout the day (not including exercise). We will need to make a generalization here, as a construction worker will burn more during the day than I will, sitting at my desk writing. Third are the calories you burn during exercise. That basic equation looks like this:

RMR + DAE + Exercise = Daily Caloric Expenditure

In order to calculate RMR and DAE, use the formulas below:

1. To calculate RMR:

Men: RMR = (9.99 × weight in kg) + (6.25 × height in cm) – 4.92×age) + 5
Women: RMR = (9.99 × weight in kg) + (6.25 × height in cm) – (4.92×age) – 161

Example for a 35-year-old/ 5'4"/120-pound woman:

> **Convert to centimeters and kilograms:**
> 5'4" = 64 inches. 64×2.54 = 162.56 cm
> 120 pounds to kg = 120/2.2 or 54.55 kg

> **Plug the converted numbers into the RMR formula:**
> (9.99 × 54.55) + (6.25 × 162.56) – (4.92×35) – 161
> (544.95) + (1,016) – (172.2) – 161 = 1,227 RMR Calories

2. To calculate the RMR + DAE:

> **Multiply RMR number by 1.2.**

Using our example:
1,227 × 1.2 = 1,472.

Note: The 1,472 amount is not in addition to the RMR, but rather the total calories needed up to this point.

3. To calculate calories burned via exercise:

Caloric expenditure is based more on distance than on pace, so if you know how far you run, you can calculate how much you have burned.

Note: Caloric expenditure is roughly 1 calorie (kcal) per kg of body weight (BW) per km run. 1 km equals 0.621 miles.

Staying with our example, if she ran 10 miles, divide that by 0.621 to get 16.1 kilometers:

Distance in km × BW = Exercise Expenditure

16.1 km × 54.55 kg = 878.26 calories burned for the run.

Now we have all the information we need to determine a total number of calories needed by our runner:

1,472 (RMR + DAE) + 878 (exercise) = 2,350 calories

As you figure out these numbers for yourself, you'll find that the total calories required won't be a static number from day to day. One major daily variable is the amount you are running. A long run day will require more calories than a rest day or shorter run (which, by the way, is a key reason that you need to take in more calories in general during marathon training than you would during 5K training). A second variable is that weight can be a factor if you lose pounds as training progresses.

Many runners cringe at the idea of counting calories. Rest assured, it doesn't have to be part of your daily routine forever, but initially, it's important to keep track in order to see what that amount of food looks like throughout the day. The goal is to get to the point where you know what to eat on what days (easy vs. intense) and what kinds of foods will do the job without you needing to count the calories in every meal and snack. These formulas are also a great reference to go back to if you change training habits, lose weight, or start to feel run down.

Table 13.1 gives a general idea of how your caloric expenditure should be broken down into a healthy, runner-friendly diet. It offers suggestions of how much you should be eating from the major food groups on a daily basis. As you get further into training, extra calories can come from sports drinks, bars, or gels consumed before, during, and after major workouts.

Consuming the Right Calories

Knowing the number of calories you should consume is just one part of the puzzle. Knowing what foods you should eat to reach that number is the next step. All calories are *not created equal*. And just as our caloric needs change based on the amount of activity we do in a day, so too will the breakdown of what types of food we need. While taking in the right calories remains vital regardless of the distance you're training for, marathon training in particular has a way of exposing deficiencies. This makes the quality of your diet that much more important.

We will explore this topic from two angles in order to demonstrate different nutritional methods. The first is more old school, involving caloric numbers and percentages. The second is more nuanced, centering on body weight and what you did during the day. The first approach is a method many of us use today and so initially may make more sense. However, as you gain confidence in your nutrition, don't hesitate to individualize your dietary intake by using the second method. The purpose of this section is to get you to think about where your calories are coming from and if those calories are helping or hurting you over time.

It's never been easier to track your calories and intake. There are a number of apps that will allow you to track all the details of your diet for free or a nominal fee. Consider investing a little money and time in tracking your eating habits. Seeing your diet in print can be a wake-up call, and can also show you places you are making mistakes and allow you to make better decisions.

Carbohydrates

There, we said it! These days, "carbohydrate" is practically a dirty word. While many are drawn to low-carb diets, we at Hansons are big proponents of carbohydrates. While your carbohydrate stores may not be a concern while training for a 5K, you are extremely limited in how far you can go without them when training for the marathon. As coaches, our goal is to help you train for and run your best first marathon and we feel strongly that carbohydrates will help you do that. In fact, when it comes to marathon nutrition, we tell runners that at least 50 percent of their diets should consist of carbs. The diet of an average runner using the Hansons programs probably falls into the range of 50–60 percent carbohydrate, whereas during the taper, carbs may be closer to 70 percent. As we will discuss later, these percentages will change based on what your training looks like. The key is getting the right carbohydrates at the right time and not confusing "sugar" as another term for "carbohydrate." The right carbohydrates are not your enemy. They won't make you fat, and they won't make you burn fat less efficiently. In fact, the opposite is true.

Over the last decade, carbs have received a bad rap from the media. But the conversation is somewhat misguided. To be sure, we are in the midst of an obesity epidemic, which places a major burden on people's health, as well as our nation's economy. And simple carbohydrates have largely contributed to this problem. But here's the caveat: There are two types of carbohydrates, simple and complex, and only one of them is detrimental to a person's health when consumed in excess. Simple carbohydrates come from refined grains, soda, candy, and other processed foods, while complex carbohydrates are contained in vegetables and whole grains, such as oatmeal and brown rice. Both types of carbohydrates play a role in the diet of an endurance athlete and will directly impact performance, but your main emphasis should be on fruits, vegetables, and whole grains. By focusing on complex carbohydrates, you will get the energy you need, as well as a number of important vitamins and minerals. As for simple carbohydrates, these are necessary for rapid absorption during exercise (or your race), as well as a way to quickly begin the refueling process after a tough workout.

Carbohydrates are an important part of an endurance athlete's diet for several reasons. From the perspective of performance, carbohydrates are utilized much faster than fat and protein. At increased intensities, carbohydrates become our sole fuel source by allowing our bodies to continue producing energy through anaerobic means once we have reached VO_2max. Meanwhile, fat is used predominantly at lower intensities because it can't keep up with high-energy demands, and protein is relied upon when carbohydrate stores are exhausted. Carbohydrates also aid in water absorption, so when you're taking in fluids during a long run, carbohydrates help the stomach empty faster, allowing the body to more efficiently utilize water. This means that fluids and carbohydrates reach their final destinations more quickly, and the faster they get there, the less likely you are to run out of energy and hit the wall.

Carbohydrates are also the primary fuel source for your brain and central nervous system. That foggy feeling or inability to focus late in a race generally stems from rapidly depleting glycogen (carbohydrate) stores. What's more, carbohydrates play a role in metabolism. You've probably heard the old saying, "Fat burns in the flame of carbohydrates." Basically, by limiting your intake of carbohydrates, you may also limit your ability to burn fat. While not proven, the theory holds that the processes that carbohydrates and fats go through to provide energy result in certain by-products that are necessary for fat to be metabolized. Research shows that the major processes will still occur, but without carbohydrates, the process is less efficient. So limiting carbohydrates limits the body's entire fueling process. Finally, your body can't store many carbohydrates, so it's important that you replenish them on a daily basis. They account for a large portion of your recommended dietary intake because without carbohydrates, you wouldn't be able to train consistently, much less run a good marathon.

Eat to Your Needs

The idea that an endurance athlete's diet needs to be 50–60 percent carbohydrates can sound overwhelming, especially when you consider that those needs change day to day, depending on your activity level. Let's break it down a little, in order to simplify the process. Look back to when we calculated all those numbers. If an easy day requires fewer calories, does it still mean that 65–70 percent of your diet that day should come from carbohydrates? We recommend that on easy and off days, you focus on taking in 3–5 grams of carbohydrate per kg of body weight. Stay on the lower end of that range if you are trying to lose weight. For SOS days and long runs, that number will be considerably higher, closer to 7–12 grams per kg of body weight. Because men tend to have more muscle mass compared to women, most women should aim for the lower end of the range, while most men should aim for the higher end of the range.

Using our earlier example of a 120-pound woman, Table 13.1 offers sample numbers:

TABLE 13.1 **CARBOHYDRATE NEEDS FOR A 120-POUND FEMALE RUNNER (EXAMPLE)**

	Grams of carbohydrates needed	Grams to calories needed	Overall daily calorie needs	% carbohydrate of overall
Easy 6 miles	218	872	2,000	44
Speed	381	1,524	2,174	70
Strength	381	1,524	2,350	65
10-mile tempo	435	1,740	2,700	65
16-mile long run	435	1,740	2,877	60

This is a rough guide based on typical mileage for speed and strength days. It gives an important glimpse into how much daily calorie needs will vary. It's also important to note that easy runs don't require as much refueling as longer or more intense days. Keep in mind that you will be doing a hard session or long run only two or three times each week. This means that four to five days each week will be off or easy. If you kept your carbohydrate intake high on all days, you could potentially start to pack on some pounds. On the flip side, it also emphasizes the importance of replenishing carbohydrates on the harder days.

If you are trying to lose weight, calorie distribution is the first place to focus. If you replenish your carbs on the days you need to, while eating the appropriate amount of carbs on easy days, you can avoid turning those unused carbs into unwanted fat storage. What is key is how you fill the other 50–60 percent of your diet on those easy and off days. We'll discuss that in the next section.

Protein

The role of protein in endurance training has evolved over time. It used to be thought of as a filler of sorts for the endurance athlete's diet. In fact, in our first book, *Hansons Marathon Method,* we recommended that protein should be just a small percentage of a marathoner's diet, approximately 10–15 percent. But now, given new information, we suggest that protein should serve a much larger role in the diet, closer to 15–20 percent, and even higher on days you don't require as many carbohydrates. As with carbohydrates, the amount of protein we need ultimately depends on what we are doing. Some data recommends taking in 0.5–0.6 grams of protein per pound of body weight, while other data recommends up to 1.5 grams per pound of body weight. One thing is for sure: How hard you train will have a significant impact on how much protein you need. Someone running 20 miles per week for 5K training will need less than someone running 50 miles per week during marathon training. While protein isn't a heavily relied upon fuel source, it plays a major role in muscle recovery. When you are training, your muscles are constantly breaking down and rebuilding thanks to proper nutrition.

Most people need only around 1 gram of protein per kilogram of body-weight per day. However, endurance athletes require more because of this constant muscle breakdown. For runners, we recommend 1.2 grams of protein per kg of bodyweight for runs of 1–1.5 hours and 1.4 g/kgBW/day for runs lasting 2–4 hours. Table 13.2 shows the average needs for runners based on weight and amount of time run.

During exercise, protein's reparative abilities are its most important benefit to you as a marathon runner—and timing is everything. By consuming protein at the same time as carbohydrates following exercise, you minimize the damage done to your muscles and speed the pace of recovery. Most importantly, protein helps you preserve lean muscle mass, which translates into better recovery and therefore, higher-quality training. When lean muscle mass is protected and maintained, there is a greater

TABLE 13.2 **PROTEIN NEEDS FOR RUNNERS**

	Average diet	1–1.5 hours	2–4 hours
100 lb. (45.5 kg)	45.5 g	54.6 g	63.7 g
125 lb. (57 kg)	57 g	68.4 g	79.8 g
150 lb. (68 kg)	68 g	81.6 g	95.2 g
175 lb. (79.5 kg)	79.5 g	95.4 g	111.3 g
200 lb. (91 kg)	91 g	109 g	127.4 g

opportunity for carbohydrates to be stored, further preserving lean muscle mass and leading to better fuel utilization during prolonged exercise. In extreme situations, that protein can be drawn upon as an energy source—but it will come from the running muscles, signaling your body's slow breakdown. If you fuel the right way, fats and carbohydrates will provide the energy you need to successfully finish the marathon, and protein will be left to assist in post-race repair.

Unless you are a vegetarian, the average person usually doesn't have a problem meeting the protein needs in his or her diet. The bigger challenge is the timing of protein intake and the source of protein intake.

Protein Pacing and Sources

Our bodies are constantly trying to balance the muscle breakdown and rebuilding process. Throughout the day, we are breaking protein down. This is attenuated every time we work out. Whenever we ingest protein, that breakdown stops and muscle protein synthesis begins. This makes doing these three things very important.

1. Eat a meal with at least some protein every 3–4 hours. If you skip breakfast, your body's lean tissue could break down and you will not be able to maintain or repair damage from your workout.

2. Have a quality protein snack before bed. If you eat dinner (with protein) at 6:30 p.m. and then sleep all night, that is 10–12 hours of no protein. If you skip breakfast as well, that time jumps to 16–18 hours without protein. You are starving your muscles!

3. Have a high-quality protein with carbohydrate after every SOS and long run. Your muscles have been damaged and taking in the protein will interrupt that process of breakdown.

If you follow these simple guidelines, you will recover faster over time, you will maintain lean muscle mass, and you'll help yourself lose the fat weight that you want to. Preserving and building your lean tissue mass is vital to overall health and running performance.

Besides just getting enough protein, it is important to get it from the right sources, such as lean red meat, poultry, fish, milk, and eggs. In addition, some people swear by protein supplements. Whey is a good supplement option. It's soluble, gets to muscles quickly, and contains all the amino acids and other nutrients that our bodies can't make on their own. Look for high-quality lactose-free sources. Another good option is casein, which acts more slowly than whey, but together they are great teammates in preventing muscle breakdown. A third choice is soy, which is loaded with quality protein, vitamins, and minerals. This option is especially good for vegans. We will discuss general supplements in more detail below.

Fats

Fats are a necessary part of a balanced diet, especially when you consider the large quantity of fat that our bodies store. Since fat has about twice as many calories per gram as carbohydrates, a little bit of fat goes a long way in keeping you feeling full. If you limit your fat intake, either you're not eating enough food in general or you're forced to eat other nutrients all day long in order to feel satiated. Fat needs in the diet are similar whether you are training for a 5K or a marathon. Most of the dietary changes a runner should make when going from shorter distance training to marathon training will involve eating more carbohydrates to replenish and more protein to repair and sustain muscle, not more fat.

Fat is also involved with the structure of cell membranes and spinal cord tissue, which can directly affect physical performance. Finally, fat is a particularly essential part of your diet because it helps the body absorb vitamins A, D, E, and K, all of which are necessary for optimal health.

In addition to contributing to overall wellness, fats help support your training and running performance. As your endurance increases, the mitochondria within the muscles grow and become denser, which gives you the opportunity to produce a greater amount of aerobic energy. This is the point at which both fats and carbohydrates can be utilized. Once the exercise intensity reaches 85 percent or higher, however, there isn't enough oxygen available to allow fat to be burned, so carbohydrates become the primary fuel source. The good news is that, while the average person switches to burning carbohydrates at around 60 percent of their maximal running intensity, endurance training can bring that percentage up a few more points. This means that your body will be able to burn fat at a higher intensity before carbohydrates take over; in practical terms, you'll be capable of running a little bit faster for a little bit longer. Despite this, we still don't need to eat large amounts of fat. For the best results, your diet should include about 20 percent fats, coming from sources such as nuts, fish, seeds, and avocados. Limit consumption of fatty meats.

Supplements

If you have your training diet dialed in, do you really need supplements? If so, which ones? While going into specific supplements is not within the scope of this book, discussing general arguments is helpful. Very few of us hit our nutritional targets every single day. Even if you eat "clean" or entirely organic, it doesn't mean that you are getting all the vitamins and minerals you need. One solution is to take a multivitamin. A quality multivitamin can help ensure you get the right nutrients on a regular basis. However, it's important to be aware that the vitamin industry is poorly regulated. One way to ensure you're actually getting what is stated on the label is to look for a seal of approval from the National Sanitation Foundation (NSF). The NSF is a third-party quality-testing institute created to protect buyers from poor products. If you choose to take a supplement, make sure it's quality or you'll literally be flushing money down the toilet.

Marathon Hydration

The human body is comprised of two-thirds water, making hydration as critical to a runner's performance as nutrition. Just as with nutrition, proper hydration becomes increasingly serious with added miles, meaning you may need to more closely monitor this during marathon training than you might have done for shorter races in the past.

Most of us are familiar with the general health benefits associated with proper hydration, but you may not know it also specifically contributes to recovery and performance. The impact of sweat loss on endurance performance may surprise you. Research has shown that a decrease in hydration stores as small as 2 percent can marginally affect physical performance. At a 3 percent loss, that impact surges to about a 5 percent decrease in VO_2max. The real race-buster is that at a 5 percent loss, we see a whopping 30 percent reduction in VO_2max. That's a major performance inhibitor! Since sweat rates can reach up to 1–2 pounds per hour on a cool, dry day, imagine the loss in hot and humid conditions. The resulting physical response to dehydration is multifaceted. Many of the effects stem from impaired cardiovascular functions via increased heart rate, decreased stroke volume, and decreased cardiac output. All of these affect a runner's VO_2max and therefore pace.

Besides the cardiac implications, dehydration leads to a number of other problems. It impairs your body's ability to dissipate heat, increasing your body temperature. Not only will this stall your performance, it will increase your risk of heat-related illnesses, such as heat exhaustion and heat stroke. Gastrointestinal distress is another symptom, which may lead you to avoid drinking more fluids, making the problem even worse. Dehydration can also cause an imbalance in electrolytes, which are critical for muscle contractions, leading to cramps, weakness, and incomplete conduction between nerves and muscles. In addition, the decreased VO_2max. will cause you to burn through your glycogen stores at a much higher rate. If this wasn't bad enough, dehydration can even result in cognitive impairment, so you may not even have the wits to pull over and stop running.

We're not looking to scare you, but we do want to emphasize the importance of hydration both in the short term during exercise, as well as the effect of dehydration over several days or weeks. When determining the appropriate fluid intake, take into account the following list of factors that affect fluid loss.

> **Ambient temperatures.** Unsurprisingly, the hotter it is, the more you'll sweat. And the more fit you are, the more you will sweat.

> **Humidity.** In some cases, this can have a larger impact than actual air temperature. Consider the 2008 Olympic marathon in Beijing, China: Temperatures were very warm, but it was not humid. The overall times were fast and even included a new Olympic record. However, two years prior, in Osaka, Japan, the World Championship

marathon was run in similar heat, but with higher humidity, and race times suffered significantly. Remember, the level of humidity close to your body can increase if you're wearing non-wicking materials next to the skin. This means that the cotton shirt you like to run in is creating a more humid environment around your body.

> **Body surface area.** Bigger runners have a higher capacity to dissipate heat, but they also have increased surface area to gain heat, especially in hot weather. In essence, the bigger you are, the more likely you are to be hotter and sweat more.

> **Condition of the athlete.** Highly trained athletes have a much better cooling potential than non-conditioned athletes.

> **Original state of hydration.** If a runner is already slightly dehydrated going into an event, he or she will reach critical points of dehydration much sooner than an athlete who is well hydrated.

While it is important to understand how fluid is lost, you'll also want to know what factors impact fluid absorption. That is, once we ingest the fluid, how does it get from the stomach to the bloodstream where we can actually use it? While carbs aid in the absorption of water, it's important to note that different types of carbs are absorbed at varying rates. Since carbohydrates are basically chains of molecules, the longer the chain, the more time it will take to exit the stomach. As scientists have begun to grasp the inner workings of this process, sports drink companies started including two lengths of chained carbohydrates in their beverages (usually dextrose and maltodextrin). With these drinks, you get the short chains that are quickly absorbed for immediate usage as well as the longer chains that assist in sustained absorption over time.

The amount of fluid you consume at any given time also influences the rate of absorption. Although larger amounts of fluids ingested at one time are absorbed more quickly, you aren't going to want to gulp down multiple cups of fluids at a single water stop during the marathon. Instead, start by consuming large amounts of fluids during the days leading up to the event and smaller quantities the day before and the morning of the race. Keep in mind that the temperature of the fluid can also increase or decrease absorption. At rest there appears to be no difference, but during exercise, cooler fluids seem to leave the stomach much faster, while room-temperature drinks are more effectively utilized.

Although you will have little control over the temperature of beverages taken from the marathon course, you do have the ability to influence other absorption-related factors, such as your own state of hydration at the start line. Once you begin running, there is no turning back to correct your hydration status. If you're dehydrated at mile 1, you will continue to be dehydrated for the entire race. The progressive nature of dehydration makes it increasingly difficult to catch up once you're at a deficit. Similarly, the faster you run, the harder it becomes for your body to absorb fluids into the bloodstream because the blood is pulled away from non-vital functions and directed toward the exercising muscles. Instead of circulating blood through the intestines and stomach, your system is working to pump blood to your legs to provide oxygen. Besides the physiological difficulties associated with absorbing fluids during fast running, there are also logistical challenges. Anyone who has ever tried to take a drink while running at a fast pace has probably found it's easier to spill it than to drink it.

Monitoring your hydration status is as important to your marathon performance as any other aspect of training. Your hydration will support you during easy runs, SOS days, and the race itself by keeping you healthy and allowing for consistent training. When it comes to mastering proper nutrition and hydration, practice makes perfect. It may take greater focus and attention in the beginning, but over time, your judgment will improve and your base of fuel-related knowledge will expand.

Hyponatremia

Hyponatremia occurs when there is an imbalance between the sodium and water contents in the blood. It tends to surface when a runner is losing a significant amount of sweat and simultaneously consuming large amounts of water. When training or racing shorter distances, the threat of dehydration is pretty minimal. However, for the marathon, we are continually told to drink more water. As a result, many runners will drink significantly more water than is necessary and then compound the problem by not including any electrolytes in the water. Since sodium is involved in nerve impulses and proper muscle function, this lack of electrolytes disrupts an important balance within the body. There are three types of hyponatremia: euvolemic, when the water content increases and the sodium content stays the same; hypervolemic, when both the sodium and water content increase, but the increase in water is far greater; and hypovolemic, when both sodium and water decrease, but sodium decreases faster. In all three instances, the concentration of sodium in the blood is diluted. It's like mixing a bottle of Gatorade, drinking half, and then refilling with just water, weakening the original mixture.

The effects of hyponatremia are very serious, as it can affect brain and muscle function to the point of coma and death. Moderation in your hydration plan is important. Stick to these guidelines.

> If your exercise session will be more than an hour long, use a sports drink.

> Know your exercise sweat rate and drink to match it. Although most people replace about 65–80 percent of their fluid losses,

some people do drink beyond that point. (You can find interactive worksheets online to help you calculate your sweat rate, for example at www.mysportscience.com.)

)	In recovery, choose drinks that contain electrolytes. Plenty of varieties offer low-carbohydrate options for daily replacement.

Eating and Drinking During Training

Pre-Workout

The hours before your workout can be the toughest time to dial in nutrition and hydration, especially if you're trying to fit in early morning runs before work. While it would be ideal for you to get up an hour before your run to take in a bit of fuel, we understand that busy runners hold sleep in high regard, especially when you're recovering from daily hard training. Every minute counts and that goes for both running and sleeping. When considering your pre-workout routine, you have to weigh the pros and cons of time-related factors. If you have to cut your slumber to five or six hours just to get up and fuel an hour before your run, you might be better off having a healthy snack before bed and getting more sleep.

Focus on pre-workout fueling on SOS workout days in particular because fuel depletion can compromise pace and performance. Easy days are less of a concern since you won't need as much fuel to execute the workout. If you're running later in the day, however, you have a greater number of fueling options from which to choose. Typically, the more time you have, the more you should eat. As your workout approaches, the goal is to get in what you need the most of, namely, carbohydrates and fluids, without filling up too much. Table 13.3 offers basic guidelines for eating before workouts.

TABLE 13.3 **PRE-WORKOUT FUEL TIMING**

Time before workout	Option	Contents
3–4 hours	Meal	Carbs, fat, protein
2 hours	Snack	Carbs, protein
1 hour	Fluids	Carbs
5–10 minutes	Fluids or energy gel	Carbs

During Workouts

A certain amount of trial and error is necessary as you fine-tune your overall fueling plan, so it is vital to test mid-run nutrition during training. The best time to practice is in workouts that exceed one hour of running; anything shorter and you likely won't need to worry about fueling. Getting this right will help you avoid both dehydration and exhaustion of those precious carbohydrate stores. While there are times when you may have to force yourself to eat and drink during a hard effort, your body will thank you on race day. There is perhaps no greater performance booster than simple calories and hydration.

Hydration will undoubtedly give you the most bang for your buck in both training and races. Not only will fluids help maintain blood-volume levels, but sports drinks can also provide crucial calories without having to add another component to your plan. Your own sweat-loss rate may vary, but on average, we lose between 2 and 4 pounds of sweat per hour. If that's not replaced, muscles receive less oxygen, less heat is evaporated, and by-products (lactic acid) accumulate in greater amounts. Among other outcomes, the body tries to compensate by making the heart beat faster. And for every 1 percent of body weight lost through dehydration, you will slow down by about 2 percent. The marathon is already hard enough, so the last thing you need is your heart thumping faster and your legs moving slower. At an 8:00-minute pace, a 2 percent loss in pace resulting from a 1 percent loss in body weight (as little as 1–2 pounds) translates into 5 lost seconds per mile. If you slow down by 2–4 percent, which is quite common, that 8:00-minute pace slows to closer to an 8:20 pace. That is the difference between a 3:29 and a 3:38 marathon finish.

Hydration is one key to your training and racing success. Here are some general rules of thumb about hydration during training.

- **Start early.** Drink within the first 10–20 minutes of running. Consider the gas tank analogy. If you have a full tank of gas, it seems to take a decent amount of time to get to a half tank. However, once you get to a half tank, that needle seems to drop a lot quicker to the quarter-tank mark. If you are already down to a half tank at 13 miles, you can expect that the tank is going to get to empty a lot sooner than the end of your long run. Start the hydration process early to keep your "gas tank" as close to full as you can, knowing that as the run goes on, it's impossible to play catch-up.

- **Drink 2–8 ounces of fluid every 15–20 minutes.** This means carrying sufficient water with you on your workout or placing it strategically beforehand.

- **Keep in mind that it's easier to drink more during the early stages of a run.** If you drink more early on and keep replacing fluids regularly, you will keep the stores topped off. This creates the fastest gastric emptying, which means more rapid absorption of water, electrolytes, and carbohydrates.

- **Count gulps.** One gulp is roughly equal to 1 ounce of fluid. Try for 4–6 gulps per water break.

- **Don't overdo it.** Downing multiple cups of water will only make you sick.

Guidelines for mid-run nutrition are similar to those for hydration. Again, fueling during workouts isn't something you need to practice during shorter runs. Practice your nutrition plans on runs longer than an hour. Gels are a popular refueling product, but other options, such as chews, are gaining a following. Glucose tablets, which diabetics use to raise their blood-sugar levels, are another alternative. They dissolve in your mouth and are a quick source of carbohydrates. Also, sports drinks will add precious calories to your overall intake, relieving the need to take in as many calories from solid foods. (Note: If you use gels or something similar, chase with water, not a sports drink.)

The faster you are running, the faster carbohydrates will be used on a per hour basis. This is true whether you are doing a speed workout or a long run. A high-intensity speed workout can deplete you as much as a 10-mile tempo. It's simply a matter of intensity over a period of time. If you are running faster than 7:00-minute mile pace, you will need 90 grams per hour to be at peak. If you are between 7:00-10:00-minute pace, your best bet is 60 grams per hour and then 30 grams per hour for pace slower than that.

An 8-ounce sports drink supplies 10–20 grams of carbohydrate. Gels provide 25 grams of carbohydrate. If you drink 8 ounces of sports beverage every 20 minutes, you get 30–60 grams per hour. So, there's a number of ways to get that desired number of grams in. In addition to fluids and gels, some runners also find calories in other types of food. It depends on what you prefer.

A calculated fueling regimen plays an important role in your mental game, as well. A solid fuel and hydration plan is a big part of your race strategy, and should be practiced during workouts. Early on in your run, having a plan helps keep you in check and focused on the task. As the miles pass, as you're consumed with how far you have left to run, put your focus on something smaller and more attainable, such as your next gel. Try to simply think about keeping your pace until the next fluid or fuel checkpoint. As you take in each gel, reset and start again. Breaking the run down into bite-sized pieces can make the distance feel a lot more achievable than if you get too focused on the entirely of the task.

Postworkout

Refueling after a workout is just as important to the quality of your next workout as your pre-workout nutrition was to the effort you just completed. Be sure not to overlook its significance. Proper postworkout fueling will help you recover from the run, maintain high levels of training, and ultimately make you a better runner. We recommend the following plan for filling up after winding down.

> For every pound of body weight lost, replenish with 20 ounces, or 2.5 cups, of water. To get an idea of how much water weight you tend to lose on a run, weigh yourself periodically throughout the first weeks of training, both before and after runs. With time you'll be able to make an educated guess about how much you should drink following a run. Calculate your sweat-loss to learn your specific needs. There are several online worksheets to help you do so.

> The initial 15–30 minutes following exercise are the most important. Immediately after your workout, take in 50–100 grams of carbohydrate along with 20–40 grams of protein. We recommend foods with a higher glycemic index, since they will get into the bloodstream and delivered to the muscles quickly. The glycemic index ranks foods on their rate of digestion. The quicker a food digests, the higher the number. My favorite post-SOS refueling is a meal-replacement shake or a bar (just make sure the protein is high quality) or chocolate milk. To make sure I get enough carbohydrates with the protein, I will have another gel or fruit (usually a banana). That gets me about 35 grams of protein and 50-plus grams of carbohydrates.

❱ Plan ahead. If you are driving to your workout, pack something to consume when you are finished rather than waiting until you return home. Start the refueling process as soon as possible.

❱ Eat a meal within the two hours following those first 30 post-exercise minutes. Oatmeal, peanut butter and a bagel, or cereal are good choices, as is anything else that contains a large amount of healthy carbs and some protein to promote muscle repair. A protein-rich drink, like chocolate milk, is a great option.

Fine-Tuning in the Final Week

Once all the hard work is done and you have cut back on both the volume and intensity of your training, spend time fine-tuning your nutritional game plan. Although by this point you have reduced your training volume, be sure to maintain a normal diet and avoid making any big changes.

The following is a guide with tips for the final days leading up to the big race.

4–7 days out from the race: Mimic your regular diet. The key is to eat to your needs. Match your intake of calories to what you are burning to avoid a big weight gain. With the reduced volume and intensity of training, you'll still be providing your body with the needed nutrients to replenish glycogen stores and repair muscle.

The last 3 days: Time to get serious about carbs. While in the first part of the week you shouldn't be gaining any weight, the last few days will probably show a couple pounds of gain due to increased carb intake. Although you might feel a little sluggish, don't panic. It's weight that will be coming off during the race. We recommend 4 grams per pound 3 days out, and 5 grams per pound 2 days out. Some men peak at about 600–700 grams. The day before the race, you have some leeway, staying somewhere between 3–4 grams per pound. Definitely don't wait until the pasta race dinner the night before to put those carbs in, because you'll be doing too little too late.

Also, be sure to hydrate throughout the entire week with electrolyte drinks. While you may not like the idea of drinking your calories, you need those extra electrolytes. Don't wait until the day prior to play catch-up.

The day before the race: Drink a healthy beverage with every snack and meal. Rather than sticking with water, mix it up with sports drinks. Avoid foods that cause gas or gastrointestinal disruption, high-fiber foods, and sugar substitutes.

Limit your alcohol intake. Eat or drink a healthy bedtime snack.

Eating and Drinking on Race Day

The primary goal the few hours before the start of the race is to top off fuel stores and stay hydrated. As for fluids, if you are a heavy sweater, consider "stocking up" on fluids 2–4 hours pre-race. The fluid you take in should include electrolytes and carbohydrates. Stop fluid intake in the last 30–60 minutes before race start in order to avoid a last-minute need for the porta potty.

Consume carbohydrates via the following guidelines.

- 4 hours prior: 200 grams

- 3 hours prior: 150 grams

- 2 hours prior: 100 grams

- 1 hour prior: 50 grams

The optimal amount of time to allow between eating and the start of the race varies based on the individual. If you don't mind waking up early, you can eat, and then return to bed. If you have a sensitive stomach, a substantial bedtime snack may be a better option. Do what works for your body.

Fueling During the Marathon

We can't stress enough how important it is to take in calories and hydrate during the race. No matter your training efforts, it could mean the difference between achieving your goal and not even being able to reach the finish line.

Minimizing fluid loss and maintaining carbohydrate intake during the race are key. Your practice during workouts, especially during long runs and tempo runs, will pay off now. The guidelines discussed for workouts should be exactly what you are trying to emulate on race day.

Like anything, fueling needs can be highly individualized, but there are general rules of thumb that will help make your marathon fueling simple and effective. For events lasting up to 2.5 hours, you're looking at 30–60 grams of carbohydrates per hour. Events lasting between 2.5 and 6 hours require greater than 60 grams per hour, up to 90 grams per hour. Those ranges depend on how much you have practiced with carbohydrates during your training. If you haven't practiced much, then trying to aim for the high end of the range will probably only leave you with stomach issues. Conversely, if you've been practicing taking in carbohydrates on tempo and long run days, your stomach will be trained to fully utilize them on race day. If this is the case, aim for the high end of the range.

The easiest way to approach fueling is to take your goal time and multiply by the number of grams that fits you. For example, if your goal is 4 hours, then multiply 4 by 60 to get 240 grams of carbohydrate in during the race. From there, you can figure how to break that down on race day.

This simple plan is based on using the race-provided sports drink and carrying your own gels:

15 minutes prior to start: 1 gel (25 grams/carbs).

Start–1 hr: 4 oz. sports drink at each aid station. If we assume regular sports drink, served in 4-oz. cups, we are looking at about 7 grams of carbohydrate per cup. If you hit a station every 2 miles, then you would encounter 3 aid stations during this hour, for a total of 21 grams from fluid.

30 minutes into race: Take another gel (25 grams/carbs).

Note: The total for the first hour is 46 grams plus the 25 grams before the start to equal 71 grams. This is on pace for 60 grams per hour.

1–2 hrs: You should hit 2–3 aid stations in this time period, for about 21 grams. One gel at the 1:15 mark and another at the 2-hour mark equal another 50 grams of carbs, for a total of 71 grams.

2–3 hrs: Drinking sports drink at the aid stations nets you another 21 grams of carbs. A gel at 2:45 adds 25 grams, for a total of 46 grams.

BUT I'M NOT HUNGRY!

It's important to stick to your fueling plan even when you don't feel you need the calories. Think back to our gas tank analogy. When you start the race, the pace should feel relatively comfortable and it will be easier to stay on point with your fueling plan. Aim to keep your schedule regardless of how comfortable you feel. The longer you can stay on schedule, the better. Eventually, you will get to a point where all your concentration is on the few feet in front of you. Your desire to take anything in will lessen. But staying vigilant in those early miles will help you head off potential issues when you're feeling tired in the latter stages of the race.

3–4 hrs: A gel at the 3:30 mark, plus fluid from each aid station, will net you about 45+ grams of carbs.

Post 4 hours: Repeat as above, with a gel at the 4:30 mark and fluid from each aid station.

Remember there is flexibility around this plan. If you are more comfortable with fluids, feel free to get more than one cup of fluid at an aid station. Or if you would prefer a gel with water instead of simply drinking a sports drink at some point, that works too. The key is knowing how many total grams you need and then figuring out what you need to carry with you and what you'll get out on the course.

As with most dietary guidelines and recommendations, the aforementioned numbers are based on averages. If a runner is very fit, lean, and muscular with a high proportion of slow-twitch muscle fibers, his or her storage capabilities may be higher. Regardless of these factors, all runners should err on the side of caution. If your stomach can tolerate the calories, then there is no reason not to provide them.

Finally, we can't emphasize enough the importance of nutritional dress rehearsals before race day. You should toe the line knowing exactly when and what you'll be eating and drinking the entire 26.2 miles.

14

SHOES AND
OTHER GEAR

SHOES ARE YOUR MOST ESSENTIAL PIECE OF GEAR, and as your mileage increases, they become even more important. Keep in mind that while a certain pair might have been fine for running a few miles a few times a week, they might not be adequate for marathon training.

Shoes are an extension of your personal biomechanics. While a few lucky runners with textbook-perfect bone and muscle structure exist, chances are you aren't among them. Most runners have at least a couple of minor imperfections, like a leg that's a little longer than the other, a fallen arch, or a weak pelvis, that predispose them to injury. Unfortunately, the more we run, the more these discrepancies come to light. That's where shoes come into play. In the same way that we preach smart training and good nutrition, we also urge runners to get fit for the right shoes. It's that important.

In this chapter, we will examine stride biomechanics, foot type, and the various components to look for in a shoe. The information will help you select the best shoe for you.

Running Stride Biomechanics

When it comes to selecting a shoe, an important factor to consider is foot strike, the point of impact when your foot hits the ground. Also important is the amount of time your foot stays on the ground with each step. With foot strike, the goal is to have brief ground contact time so that you experience minimal braking force (which slows you down and is jarring to your body), but not so brief that the maximal force used to move the body forward is compromised. It may not seem like foot strike could have a significant overall effect on performance, but in the long run, it makes a big difference. If you run 5 kilometers in 30 minutes, you will take a whopping 5,400 steps. If you could decrease your footstrike time by just 1/100th of a second, you would run a whole minute faster over those 5 kilometers. Extrapolate that to the marathon and you're talking about potentially shaving minutes off your time, merely by striking more efficiently.

Although researchers agree on many aspects of footstrike biomechanics, there is much debate over the ideal place to land: the heel, midfoot, or forefoot are all contenders. For all the controversy, there is relatively little research on the topic and the studies that have been conducted should be approached with caution, as there is much speculation about the results. One of the more reliable studies, conducted in 2007 (Hasegawa, et al., *Journal of Strength and Conditioning*, 2007 (21), 888-893), looked at the footstrike patterns of elite runners during a half-marathon race. The results showed that nearly 75 percent landed on their heels, while 24 percent landed midfoot, and just 1 percent were forefoot strikers. It should also be noted that 60 percent of the first 50 finishers of the race were midfoot strikers. This was followed by a study in 2013 (Kasmer, et al., *International Journal of Sports Physiology and Performance*, 2013, 8, 286–292) that looked at nearly 2,000 marathoners and found about 93 percent of the runners had some variation of heel strike. However, it's important to note that this study looked only at the 8K mark of a marathon; a lot can happen between 5 miles and the next 20 miles! However, in 2011 Larson, et al. (*Journal of Sports Science*. 2011 Dec;29(15):1665–73. Epub 2011 Nov 18.), found that even the small group of forefoot strikers early in a race had switched to rearfoot striking by about the 20-mile mark.

Where you strike in relation to your body is also key. For many years, runners were told to land each foot directly underneath their body, but new evidence shows that this is just as inefficient as the foot landing way out in front of you. Current research suggests that a runner should be landing nearly flat-footed in front of the waist with their knee slightly bent.

The key here, though, is that two runners could technically be heel strikers, but with totally different outcomes. To fully understand this, we have to move beyond just what part of the foot is hitting the ground.

Since the research is somewhat unreliable in even categorizing the various types of footstrike, it is more productive to look at the matter in terms of where the foot is landing relative to your body, not what part of the foot hits the ground first. The biggest mistake runners make is attempting to increase stride length. This often leads to overstriding, which means you're likely landing on your heels far out in front of your body, thereby creating a braking motion which forces your legs to absorb more shock. Since this increases the time you are in contact with the ground, your pace will also slow. If you focus on landing underneath your center of gravity, however, you'll avoid all of these things.

While the verdict is still out in the academic world, we recommend simply proceeding with training and not becoming too preoccupied with altering your natural form. There are, however, a couple practical tips concerning footstrike that may help you run more efficiently. First, avoid overstriding. The consensus seems to be that if your stride rate is less than 160 steps per minute, then you are likely overstriding. The solution is to increase in your rate by 5–10 percent. From my experience, leaning forward slightly from the ankles puts your center of gravity a little more forward. To help with your stride rate, use one of the number of apps that work like metronomes, or find music that is a specific number of beats per minute. Another suggestion is decreasing the drop of your shoe, which we will discuss later in this chapter.

Foot Type

The shape of your feet should play a role in your shoe-selection process. Among the many shapes and sizes of human beings, there are three major foot types: Flat arches, high arches, and medium arches.

The flat foot, although not the most common, is definitely the most troublesome. In addition to having a flatter arch, flat feet are often accompanied by ankles that lean inward toward one another. If you have this type of foot, you'll land on the outsides of your feet when running, and as you proceed through the footstrike your ankles will roll inward. This is referred to as overpronation. Some amount of pronation is normal, as the foot naturally rolls inward, reducing shock and giving the body leverage to push off the ground. However, when flat-footed runners overpronate, they often experience an increase in certain overuse injuries. The main problem is that their feet tend to be too flexible, cushioning the blow of the foot slamming into the ground, but also providing little leverage to carry the body through the striking motion to assist in pushing off from that step. This excessive motion leads to a host of rotational forces applied to the foot, ankle, shin, and knee, creating issues like tendonitis, plantar fasciitis, and Achilles tendonitis. As you may have guessed, this foot type requires a very specific shoe to alleviate these problems and allow for normal running.

The second foot type is the high arch. Like the flat-footed runner, a runner with this foot type also lands on the outside of the foot, but instead of rolling inward, remains there all the way through toe-off. While the flat foot offers great natural cushioning, but is a poor lever for pushing off, the reverse is true for the high-arched foot. Along with high arches comes inflexibility, so the feet are unable to do a good job of absorbing the forces that running imposes on the body. Since all of the weight is put on the outside of the foot during ground contact, even the toe-off is somewhat limited, as it can't take full advantage of the big toe as a lever to push off. Ironically, this motion, called underpronation or supination, can lead to some of the same injuries as overpronation, but for different reasons. While rotational forces tend to be the cause of injuries in flat-footed runners, poor shock absorption is the plight of supinators. In addition, this foot type may also lead to a greater number of issues with the iliotibial band, the long band of tissue that stretches from the pelvis down to the knee joint.

The final foot type is the medium (neutral) arch. This type is the least common. The lucky runner with this foot type has a footstrike that begins at the middle to the outside of the heel and then gently rolls to the middle of the foot, continuing to use the leverage of the big toe, maximizing toe-off. Although the biomechanics may be better, a medium-arched runner still runs the risk of injury by running in a shoe that is either too supportive or not supportive enough.

Each biomechanical difference comes with its own set of unique problems, making it important to choose a shoe that is made for your arch type.

Shoe Construction

Having a good grasp on the various components that are used to create running-specific footwear will also help you choose wisely. The main pieces are the outsole, midsole, last, heel counter, and the upper.

Outsole: The bottom of the shoe is called the outsole, or tread. Until recently, the outsole did little more than provide traction, with the only variation being the type of rubber used. Now, however, there are a growing number of technologies used for outsoles. Instead of one piece of rubber, the outsoles are often broken into basic pods for the heel and forefoot, which saves weight. Also, rather than rubber, today's companies are relying on new materials, like silica, which are said to provide better traction in wet conditions, and are more environmentally friendly. Outsole technology has also improved in terms of the general wear of the shoe, so you will get more miles out of a pair of shoes. In fact, for most runners, the midsole breaks down well before the outsole.

Midsole: The midsole is where most of the action occurs from a biomechanical standpoint. In recent years, midsole materials such as ethylene vinyl acetate (EVA) and air pockets have been replaced with new technologies that are more resilient, lighter, and biodegradable. Cushioning technology has also improved, allowing the shoes to absorb forces more readily and last up to 15 percent longer, and even store and return energy.

While all midsoles contain some level of cushioning, the amount of support varies. Some shoes contain a denser midsole to provide more support, including dual-density and tri-density materials. This type of midsole helps to keep an overpronating foot in a more neutral position, but also adds weight to the shoe. Different shoe models contain varying amounts of these materials, leading to a wide variety of stability and weight options. To spot a shoe that contains a denser midsole, look for a gray area that comprises part of the medial side (inside) of the midsole. Other pieces are sometimes added for extra support, such as roll bars, which make for an even stiffer, controlled shoe. The more you pronate, the more these extra components make sense. While most shoe companies are still producing shoes with these stability components, the trend now seems to be shifting away from traditional correction and more toward guiding the foot into the right position.

When you buy a good pair of running shoes, the midsole is where your money is going. Instead of looking at the tread in determining whether your shoes need to be replaced, it is more important to consider the number of miles you've run in the shoe and the wear and tear on the midsole. Despite all the technological advances, shoes still break down. As soon as the midsole is past its prime, you're at risk for injury.

Last: The last is the actual shape of the shoe. There are three basic lasts: Straight, curved, and semi-curved. Each of these three varieties is correlated with different foot types to control motion and offer optimal cushioning. A straight last is the best foundation for an overpronating runner because it helps control the excessive inward rolling that characterizes the motion of a flat-footed runner, and also provides better toe-off. A curved last offers just the opposite. Instead of being symmetrical, it is severely curved along the medial side of the shoe where the arch sits. A curved last is built for supinators to help deal with the poor natural cushioning by promoting a slight inward roll. Finally, a semi-curved last is a hybrid between the curved and the straight varieties. This is tailored to runners with a medium (neutral) arch, offering some rigidity while also allowing for natural pronation. In recent years more "blended" types of platforms have entered the market.

Heel counter: You can't see the heel counter, but it is a unit that hugs the heel to minimize motion in the ankle. Since some runners need this type of control and others don't, there are varying levels of heel-counter stability, with the most flexible shoes having no heel counter at all.

Upper: The material that covers the top of the foot is known as the upper. Usually made of a highly breathable nylon mesh, a good upper permits sweat and water to be wicked away from the feet, keeping them cool and dry. If you live in an area with cold weather, look for uppers that provide more weather-resistant capabilities to keep snow and slush out of the shoe. Lacing patterns on uppers also vary, some helping to hug the arch or provide a bit of extra support. The newest trend in uppers is using fewer pieces of material, with some models now just a single piece of material, and some companies are even dabbling in 3D printing of uppers.

Shoe Type

We are living in a transitional time for shoes. While traditional models remain, trends are shifting with new technologies. For several decades, there were few innovations in running footwear, but the book *Born to Run,* published in 2009, changed the running shoe game. Namely, the minimalist movement was born. Traditionally, shoes had a 10–12 millimeter drop from heel to toe, but the minimalist movement encouraged people to run barefoot, or in shoes with a zero-millimeter drop. Many runners tossed out their traditional sneakers in favor of zero-drop models. The trend spawned a new era in shoe design. But by 2014, the trend was slowing, with one of the original minimalist shoe producers, Vibram, settling a class action lawsuit for false health claims. Today, the minimalist market is a fraction of what it was in 2010. However, there was some good to come out of all of that. While going from a 10–12-mm to 0-mm drop is not advisable for most people, it did force shoe companies to take a close look at how they were developing shoes in terms of cushioning and structure. Today, heel drops in shoes are smaller, cushioning technologies have improved, and shoe weights have been reduced across the board.

Shoe Categories

Walking into a running shoe store and seeing the countless styles and types of sneakers displayed on the shoe wall can be intimidating. Understanding your options will go a long way toward helping you make your best selection.

Let's start by looking at the three main shoe categories: Motion control, neutral, and stability. We will then discuss specific types of shoes, including minimalist shoes, max cushion shoes, lightweight trainers, and racing flats.

Motion control: This shoe is designed for the flattest of feet. A typical motion control shoe is build atop a straight last, has a dual density midsole from the heel to beyond the arch, a plastic roll bar in the heel and arch, and a stiff heel counter. With all of the extras, these shoes aren't your lightest option, but they are good at their main job, which is to prevent overpronation.

Neutral: These shoes are best suited to a runner with high arches. They are built on a curved last with loads of cushioning, no dual density midsole materials, and a minimal heel counter. This type of footwear provides cushioning and flexibility without tipping the scales.

Stability: The stability category is for neutral and mildly overpronating "normal" runners. The last is typically semi-curved with some dual-density midsole technology, a flexible forefoot, ample cushioning, and a mild heel counter. This type of shoe provides a middle-of-the-road option for a runner who needs a slight amount of support without sacrificing cushioning.

Lightweight: Lighter weight shoes combine features of a regular running shoe and a racing flat. They are lightweight versions of a neutral shoe, but with features that provide support. Although these shoes are a couple ounces lighter than the other categories, they shouldn't be worn exclusively in training. Some runners, however, will find them a good option for certain SOS workouts, especially speed and strength work. If you're not ready for a true racing flat, you might want these for a lighter shoe to race in. They provide sufficient cushioning and support while feeling much lighter than traditional trainers.

Minimalist: Minimalist footwear offers little if any cushioning or protection for the feet, so you feel as if you're running barefoot. As discussed above, the minimalist movement flooded the market, peaked, and has since settled back into a niche market of the running shoe community. However, it is worth looking a little closer at the debate so that you can decide if this is something you want to try.

The premise of minimalism includes two basic ideas: (1) You should wear the least amount of shoe that you can tolerate without getting hurt and (2) by wearing less shoe, you strengthen your feet and improve your running stride. Minimalist advocates often argue that our ancestors were made to run barefoot, so we should get back to basics and do the same. However, we live in a much different world from our Paleolithic forefathers and mothers, and wear shoes from the time we are very young, so we need a transition from wearing shoes to going barefoot. Most proponents of minimalism suggest taking a gradual approach to decreasing the amount of shoe over the course of several months. If you are wearing a stability model, for instance, you should not go directly to a minimalist shoe, but rather use a lightweight trainer before moving to minimalist or "barefoot" footwear. This allows the bones and soft tissues to gradually adjust to the minimalist footwear. Even after you have fully transitioned, we don't recommend wearing this type of shoe every day for regular training, but rather, as a training supplement to be worn periodically.

With so many options and hybrids now on the market, a runner may not need to seek out specific minimalist shoes. A lightweight trainer or racing flat may be a good compromise if you wear these lighter shoes only once or twice per week. This allows you to adjust to the minimalist properties, while still letting you recover from workouts in your regular training shoes.

Maximalist: The pendulum swings both ways, and to counter the minimalist movement we now have the maximalist movement. Both ends of the spectrum agree that having less heel drop in a shoe is a good thing. But while minimalists approach this by cutting out all excess material and cushioning, the maximalist approach is the opposite. The shoe still has less of a drop (sometimes even a 0 mm drop), but instead of a stripped-down midsole, there is lots of cushioning. Many runners say the cushioning is gentler on their joints and allows for more enjoyable running.

The Price of Proper Footwear

As the aforementioned discussion highlights, not all shoes are created equal. Like buying a car, the more features you want or need, the more you're going to

SHOULD I ROTATE SHOES?

If possible, yes. A shoe's cushioning compresses, and when it's used every day, that compression doesn't have a chance to bounce back. If you rotate your shoes, the shoes can actually recover on their "off day." This increases the life of the shoe. One method some runners use is to have a pair of everyday training shoes in addition to a pair of lightweight trainers or racing flats for their speed, strength, and tempo work. Another option, especially for Just Finish or From Scratch marathoners, is to have a regular pair of trainers as well as a pair of maximalist shoes that you can wear a couple days per week when you feel like you need a little extra recovery. If you go with two pairs of shoes, make sure to rotate them so you get consistent use out of both.

pay. Remember, however, that shoe type should guide your decision, not how much they cost. The most expensive shoe is not necessarily the best for you. Consider your specific needs and make an informed decision.

There are three basic price points: entry level, mid-grade, and the Cadillac.

Entry level: Your cheapest option, these shoes offer the basics, but not much else. They are great for someone just getting into the sport, especially those who aren't sure they'll continue running. Most entry-level shoes are made with cushioning in the heel but not the forefoot. They are noticeably less responsive and just don't feel as comfortable as high-end models. Even still, these shoes are reliable, well constructed and get the job done. They will also be the cheapest way to get out of a running shop, retailing at around $100. While there are less expensive sneakers that can be found at big box athletic stores, we never recommend choosing anything below this category.

Mid-grade: Models that fall into this category offer the basics plus a few extras, such as full-length cushioning, better midsole material, a more responsive feel, and an enhanced overall fit. They usually retail between $110 and $120. A blend of luxury and functionality, this category of shoe will be able to withstand a few more miles than the entry-level shoes.

Cadillac: Shoes in this category have all the bells and whistles in terms of the latest technology and are often a company's premier model. While you may experience sticker shock, thanks to prices that can range from $140 to $160, many of these shoes claim to last a lot longer. So, if you stay healthy longer and your shoes last longer, these shoes may actually be cheaper in the "long run."

How to Choose a Shoe

When you're ready to buy a shoe, you will be better served going to a running specialty store rather than selecting a shoe off the Internet. Fit is everything, and you are far more likely to get it right the first time if you have a knowledgeable employee assisting with the fitting process. Selecting the right shoes is like putting together pieces of a puzzle; a well-trained employee will help you connect the dots and make a good choice. When you go to the store, bring your old running shoes if you have them and be ready to answer questions about your training and past running experience. You might be asked about past injuries, your training plans, or what you liked and didn't like about your current shoes.

The running store specialist may examine the wear pattern on the bottom of your old shoes to get a general idea of foot strike. If you tend to grind down the entire medial (inside) side of the tread, you're likely overpronating and need more support than that shoe offers. Conversely, if the outside edge is worn, you're probably supinating and need less support and more cushioning. If your wear pattern is even, you're probably in the correct shoe category. It is important to keep in mind that this isn't an exact science. If you've gone through 10 versions of the same model and haven't had any issues with injuries, stick with what you know works, regardless of the wear pattern on the bottom of the shoes.

In most running specialty shops, the employee will ask to observe your gait. Many running establishments have treadmills and cameras that capture images of the motion of your feet when walking and running. When you play the video in slow motion, you can see exactly how you are striking. Even without the technology, an experienced employee can watch you walk or run and get a good idea of what type of shoe you should be in.

Once you are presented with several options of shoes that are appropriate for your feet, you only need to decide which pair is the most comfortable. In running shoes, size definitely matters, and you may wear a half or even whole size larger than your dress shoe. When you put the shoes on, consider these factors.

Heel: The heel should provide a snug fit with little to no slippage.

Toe box: There should be some room in the toe box, in both length and width. Your toes should have room to splay out and push off when you're running, but you don't want so much room that your feet slide around.

Timing: Try to go to the store around the same time of day you'd normally run, as your feet swell during the day. What feels like the right size in the morning can feel too tight after a day spent on your feet.

The final decision comes down to how the shoe fits your foot. If you have three choices from the same category and price range, it is likely any of them will do the job. Choose the one that feels the best. Remember to select your shoes based on function, not fashion.

When to Replace Shoes

You might assume you can purchase a new pair of shoes at the beginning of your marathon training and wear them all the way through to race day. But a pair of shoes should carry a runner only 350–500 miles, depending on the shoe, body type, and running style. The From Scratch program has you running about 700 total miles over 18 weeks of training, putting anyone who trains with that plan well beyond a shoe's expiration date. Other plans have even higher mileage. In reality, you will need two pairs to get you through training and the race itself.

Consider being fitted for one pair, trying them out for a few weeks and then deciding whether to purchase an identical pair or a different model. If you love the first pair you bought, make sure that the model hasn't changed when you go to buy the next pair. Although the name may be the same, models can differ significantly from one season to the next, bringing along changes to the fit that may not jibe with your preferences and overall comfort.

Race-Day Kicks

Your first run in a new pair of shoes most certainly should not be on race day. While most shoes are ready to be worn right out of the box and require little-to-no break-in time, it is important to make sure that the pair of shoes that you'll be wearing for 26.2 tough miles are comfortable. You could wear 11 pairs of the same model and never have an issue, but you still need to give your body time to react to a new shoe. As a shoe slowly breaks down, your foot adjusts to its changing make-up. But when you lace up a new pair right off the store shelf, your feet have to make an adjustment to the more substantial thickness of the midsole and shape of the upper. The shoes you race in should have enough mileage to have that familiar feel, but not so many miles that they are beginning to break down. For most, this falls between 50 and 100 miles, or 2–3 weeks before the race.

When selecting a race-day shoe, most runners opt for a model in which they can also log plenty of training miles. While choosing a lighter shoe, or racing flat, for race day might sound appealing, this is not the best course for every runner. Remember, you are going to be on your feet for a long time—significantly longer than any of your training runs. A slightly bulkier shoe with cushioning can take the brunt of the force upon each foot strike. Racing flats are lighter for a reason. In place of cushioning and support comes a lighter and faster-feeling shoe. Since fatigue has a detrimental effect on running mechanics and running economy, you become more susceptible to injury as you tire, and it may be risky not to have that extra cushioning and support. Why sacrifice a few ounces when that may ultimately take a toll on your biomechanics?

We suggest that the cutoff for wearing racing flats is 3:10 for the marathon. Those slower than that should wear regular shoes and those faster might consider racing flats. A middle ground for runners who want to lighten up but still need some support and cushioning is a lightweight trainer. This category of shoe is a great transitional option between a regular training shoe and a racing flat. While not as substantial as an everyday training shoe, they offer enough support and cushioning for limited use, such as in a marathon. With these, you save a couple ounces of shoe weight without running the risk of injury.

Apparel

What you wear on race day will depend on both weather and what you have worn in training. A running cap may be a perfect training accessory for a rainy, cool training day in March, but during your race in July, it may do nothing but trap heat. The following are some basic guidelines to keep in mind when choosing your race-day ensemble.

Avoid cotton: Instead of helping to wick moisture and heat away from your body, cotton traps heat and absorbs sweat, creating a humid environment close to your skin. This can lead to both chafing and blisters. No cotton socks, shorts, pants or shirts.

Dress down: Pretend its 20 degrees warmer than it actually is when choosing your outfit. If it's 40 degrees out, dress like it is 60. You may be chilly the first mile, but once you start generating heat, you will warm up quickly.

True cost: Consider cost per wear when purchasing running clothing. It's not about the initial investment, but how much wear are you going to get out of it. Good running apparel is quite durable and will last several seasons.

Try it on: Sometimes seams rub, shorts are an awkward length, or the cut of a shirt is uncomfortable. Try it before you buy it to feel how it fits.

Whatever you choose to wear on race day, make sure to take it for a test run first. Ideally, you should wear the outfit on a longer training run so you are sure that with time and increased sweat output, the materials don't cause any problems. After all the hard training you've put in, the last thing you want is to have a wardrobe malfunction on the big day.

Gadgets

We live in a world of activity trackers, sleep trackers, recovery trackers, power meters, GPS devices, heart rate monitors, and hydration trackers. I find that these gadgets can take some of the joy out of running, and when you become over-reliant on this type of data, running intuition can be dampened. With that said, I know that many people love data. And there can be great benefit in using certain devices in certain situations. There is a time and a place for everything, including technology.

It is our hope that by closely following our programs, you'll learn the basic principles of training and reach top fitness. An important by-product of achieving those things is a well-honed sense of body awareness, pace, and effort. If you're zoning out and relying 100 percent on your watch to tell you how hard you're working, you won't learn those things. So when it comes to technology, a GPS watch may be all you need. GPS data is great for tracking your long runs and hard workouts and provides important indicators of progress. On other days, you can simply leave it behind. The key is not to be too dependent on the watch. Feel free to mull over the data when you finish your workout, but try to focus on putting one foot in front of the other while you're out on the running trails.

Stepping Up . . . and Beyond

15

NAVIGATING THE LAST SIX WEEKS

WHEN YOU'RE RIGHT IN THE MIDDLE OF TRAINING, it's easy to go on autopilot for a while. But as race day draws near, runners often begin to feel the full weight of their marathon goal. It's that moment when you recognize you're really going to do this: run 26.2 miles on foot, preferably without stopping. Rest assured, you aren't alone if you experience fear, uncertainty, and maybe even dread. In fact, such feelings are so common that we've devoted an entire chapter to helping you navigate the final month and a half of training. Hopefully the coming pages will address any final questions or concerns regarding what you're about to become: a marathoner.

6 Weeks to 2 Weeks Out from Goal Race

This 4-week block is a critical time in your training. It is also the point when runners begin to question if their goals are attainable. This is totally normal. At this point in your training, aches and pains, accompanied by cumulative fatigue from training, are beginning to add up. You may ask yourself, "How am I going to manage 26.2 miles at this pace?" This question can set into motion a cascade of self-doubt and negative self-talk. And, as self-fulfilling prophecies go, the less we believe in our abilities, the more likely we are to fall apart on race day.

Why do we get this way? This cycle is usually triggered not by our minds, but by our bodies. Four common culprits can leave a runner feel wholly worn out going into the final block of training.

Shoes: As discussed, most shoes are good for 300–500 miles. Let's assume you start your training off with a brand-new pair of shoes. You proceed to put 12 weeks of training on that pair of shoes. That's at least 400 miles—or more, depending on your plan—and you still have six weeks to go! So if you feel aches and pains starting to pop up, first check the mileage on your shoes.

Training: This four-week block is the toughest part of the training. The SOS days are the hardest and the mileage is the highest. It probably is the most running you have ever done. You are bound to feel a few new aches and pains. Reassure yourself that this is normal and part of the adaptation process—to a point. Be watchful that those part-of-the-process aches and pains don't turn into injuries.

Intensity: Some runners have the mindset, "If fast is good, faster is better," and they run too aggressively early in their training. Over time, this adds up, and at some point, something's got to give. Remember, you aren't going into every workout 100 percent recovered, so if you make it harder than it needs to be, you simply dig a hole of fatigue deeper and deeper. You can't go back in time and run with less intensity, but you can focus on the now. Let your new challenge be to listen to your body and pull back as necessary, especially on easy days.

Recovery: If you haven't mastered the basics of recovery yet, now's the time you will really feel the lack. Put energy into your recovery, making sure that sleeping, rehydrating, and refueling are priorities from here on out.

2 Weeks from Race Day: The Taper

Much of the last two weeks of training is mental. The hay is in the barn, so to speak, and now it's all about trusting that the magic will happen. Your fitness is there, so you just need to recover from the cumulative fatigue. That is where the taper comes in.

But tapering can be scary. The final two weeks before your race involves reduced mileage and intensity, and brings along with it a fear of the unknown. It's easy to get spooked. You've invested significant time, money, and effort into this event. If it doesn't go well, then it's not like a 5K, where you can just find another race the next week. There's a lot riding on marathon race day. Some common thoughts during the taper period include:

"I'm going to get fat!"

"I'm going to lose all my fitness!"

"Where did all these aches and pains come from?"

"I'm not backing my training off enough!"

The truth is, you're probably not gaining weight, you aren't losing fitness, and you're not injured. Our minds play tricks on us during this time.

The weeks of training that you did up to now have left your body feeling fatigued. The taper is designed to allow you to fully recover from all your hard training and reap the fitness that you've gained. Tapering is all about adjusting the frequency, intensity, duration, and type of running that you do. And it's an art as much as a science. Decrease too much at one time and you get sluggish. Decrease too many of the variables for too long and you pass the point of recovering fully and go into detraining, losing those hard-fought fitness gains.

A good taper should be gradual, not drastic. Our programs gradually step you down in mileage and intensity so that you don't shock your body by radically decreasing workload. Here are the taper's basic guidelines:

1. Keep the taper between 10 days and 2 weeks. Longer than that and you get sluggish and risk losing fitness.

2. Do your last really hard workout about 7–10 days out.

3. Keep the frequency of training days up.

4. Reduce your volume by about 25 percent of peak mileage during the first week of the taper and then 40–50 percent the second week (not including the race).

A properly executed taper can yield a performance increase of 0.5 to 3 percent. For a 4-hour marathoner, that puts you at about 3:58 to 3:52. Does this mean that if you are training for a 4-hour marathon that now you can run 3:55 because you tapered? Unfortunately, no. But it will make a pace that felt hard during your tempo runs feel doable in the race. A proper taper that balances workload and rest can leave you feeling like a superhero come race morning.

The Last Few Days

Over the years, the Hansons coaches have adopted the saying "worry early." What we mean by that is that it is important to tend to race-day details in advance to limit unnecessary stress on the big day. You've committed to 18 or more weeks of hard training, early mornings, skipped social events, and other sacrifices; don't blow it by neglecting to iron out the particulars of the race well in advance.

There is no strategy that will completely eliminate race-day nerves, but there are certain steps that can put you ahead of those who aren't prepared.

HOW DO I HANDLE STRENGTH AND MOBILITY TRAINING DURING MY TAPER?

If you are doing a core routine or a bodyweight program, you should continue it during the taper. Consider scaling back to 3 days per week during the first week of the taper, and do your final session 3–4 days out from the race. The same is true for any aerobic crosstraining you are doing. Mobility work such as foam rolling and dynamic warm-ups can be done all the way up until the day before the race. Just keep it moderate. If you are doing heavy strength training, I'd scale back to once or twice during the first week of the taper and then nothing heavy the week of the race.

From your pre-race meal to where you'll meet your family at the finish to what shoes you're going to wear, planning ahead will go a long way toward keeping you calm when it matters. Going into race weekend, your plan should be rehearsed and ready to be put into motion. When you're relaxed at the start line, you're less likely to make mistakes in the early stages of the race, keeping you focused and ready to follow protocol.

Don't underestimate the amount of planning a marathon requires. Consider the following factors as you make your arrangements prior to race morning, remembering that your marathon will only be as good as your pre-race preparation, whether that is the training itself or getting to the start line on time.

Travel

If you are traveling to a race, be aware that crossing times zones can get tricky. While crossing a single time zone won't have much impact on your daily patterns, going from coast to coast can definitely play tricks on your circadian rhythms. The general rule of thumb is that you need a day for every 90 minutes you gain (east to west travel) and a day for every 60 minutes you lose (going west to east). In other words, you will adapt more quickly traveling west than you will east. Where it gets even more complicated is traveling overseas.

A traveling runner should aim to get on the schedule of the relevant time zone as soon as he or she lands. So if you arrive at your destination in the evening, then get right into what you would do in the evening. Eat a dinner that's got a bit of carbs in it and darken your hotel room. Both of these will help put you into a sleepier mood. If you arrive in the daytime, then even if you are tired, you need to be active. Maybe save your run for when you arrive. Make your room bright. Do what you need to do to stay awake until it is time to go to bed for the night.

Some find it easier to sign up for a local race in order to avoid the extra costs and hassle associated with traveling. But even if your race is local, you still might want to consider getting a hotel room. Staying at a conveniently located hotel the night before means you can walk to the start line the next morning. There are a couple of advantages to this strategy. It allows you to get a bit more shut-eye before rising for the big day, and if you tend to get stressed by the crowds and chaos surrounding race morning, you might find that walking a few blocks to the start line eases your anxiety. If you prefer to sleep in your own bed the night before, be sure to leave early enough to get to the start. While you may live only 15 minutes from where the race begins, traffic and parking can be challenging in any city during marathon morning. Consider having someone drop you off so you don't have to figure out where to park your car.

Spectators

Most marathoners welcome a friendly face along the course. Not only does it break up the monotony, it also gives you something to look forward to as you grind through the miles. Review the course map and figure out the best plan for friends and family to view the race. Not only do you want your fans and supporters to see you as much as they can, but it can also be a help to you. When my wife ran the Boston Marathon, I took the train out to the 16-mile mark. Ahead of time, we'd figured out where I'd stand so she knew what side of the road I'd be on. When she saw me, she tossed me the empty fuel bottles she was carrying and I gave her two new ones. This allowed her to get the fluids she wanted without carrying more than necessary, in addition to a few important words of encouragement.

Study the Course

Know the course. If your race is local, consider running sections of the course so you know what to expect come race day. Training on the route lets you learn the turns, the hills, and other details. With familiarity comes calm and control. The elite athletes in the Hansons-Brooks Distance Project often travel to the location of an upcoming race in order to run the course a few times before the big day. Doing this early in the training segment allows us to alter what and where we do our training to be fully prepared for the course. If you don't have the luxury of running the course prior to competition, check the official marathon website, YouTube, and the blogosphere for course tours, an elevation profile, and other insights.

Race Weekend

Sightseeing

As discussed in Chapter 10, resist the desire to be a tourist before your race. The last thing you want to do is to be on your feet constantly in the 36–48 hours before your goal race. But it's no fun sitting in a hotel room for a few days. A short walk or bike ride is fine; just don't find yourself on a citywide walking tour. Consider scheduling an extra day after your race and get some touring in. Heck, the post-race walk might even make your tired legs feel better.

The Race Expo

Most race expos are akin to bustling flea markets, and it's very tempting to wander the aisles, browsing the latest running shoes, gear, and goodies. But you should avoid spending a lot of time on your feet at the expo, a common mistake runners make. In awe of the pageantry surrounding the big event, they walk around on hard concrete floors in a convention hall instead of sitting on a couch or bed, resting. For most Sunday marathons, the expo is open Friday and Saturday. If you are able, go during your lunch hour on Friday and pick up your packet. This keeps you from lingering too long and allows you to have a relaxed pre-race day. If you can't make it to the expo until the day before the race, go as early as possible to avoid the crowds and then get out of there so you can go put your feet up.

Pre-Race Dinner

Whether you're attending the race's organized pre-race dinner or staying home to eat, the guidelines are the same. Most important, carbo-loading doesn't mean eating four plates of spaghetti and three loaves of bread. Eat a healthy, regular-size meal, high in easily digestible carbohydrates. The main goal is to top off your glycogen stores before the race. This meal should cap off a week of balanced eating as suggested in the nutrition chapter; otherwise, your pre-race dinner won't make much difference. Test your meal choices ahead of time by eating the same meals leading up to your long runs so you know what to expect on race day. Additionally, while hydration is an ongoing process, be sure you use the day before the race to continue taking in water and sports drinks. Proper hydration takes time and should be tended to throughout the week.

Before Bed

Use the evening before the race to get organized. Your race bag should be packed and ready to go, the timing chip already fastened to your shoe-laces, your clothes laid out, and your water bottle full. When you head to bed, sleep may be fairly hard to come by. Don't fret if you are tossing and turning; you should have banked plenty of rest over the past 10 days. If you do find yourself awake, consider grabbing an evening snack, like a meal replacement bar or protein shake with carbohydrates in it. While this isn't necessary, the body burns through about half of the glycogen stored in the liver during the overnight hours. By eating a late-night snack, you further reduce how much you need to replace in the morning, potentially avoiding stomach upset. If you tend to get especially nervous right before a race, this is a good way to consume calories before the jitters set in. Instead of needing 300–500 calories in the morning, you may be able to reduce that to just 100–200 calories to top off glycogen stores.

16

RACE DAY!

THE BIG DAY HAS FINALLY ARRIVED. After all that build-up of anticipation, it's time to put your marathon race plan into action. If you've followed our advice from previous chapters and made your preparations ahead of time, many race-day particulars will run on autopilot. This helps reduce anxiety on what can already be a stressful day. To take the guesswork out of it for you, we've laid out a step-by-step account of what race morning should look like. As with everything else, make sure you practice these things prior to the big day.

Race Morning

If you wake up three hours or more before the race, you can eat a normal breakfast, such as a bagel with peanut butter, a banana, and coffee or juice. Any closer to gun time and you need to eat conservatively. Within a few hours of the start, eat less solid food and mostly carbohydrates. With an hour to go, stick with something like an energy gel, which will satiate you for a short time but won't give you a full feeling.

Begin measuring your liquid intake by sips, not ounces. You don't want to have water sloshing around in your stomach the first half of the race. Try to have an idea of how long you are going to be standing in the corral at the start. Sometimes runners can be there upward of an hour waiting to cross the start line. Bring fluids with you to the corral, sip to keep things topped off, and know where the portajohns are.

In addition to what you're putting in your body, consider what you're putting on your body. Check the weather forecast for before and during the race. You may well stand in the start corral for 30 minutes or more, so you'll want to be prepared. Conditions can be significantly cooler in the morning. It's a good idea to layer in order to stay warm prior to the start and then shed garments as you warm up during the race. Wear what you're willing to lose. For your bottom layer, sport your regular running gear with the race number attached, but on the top, wear an old pair of sweatpants or sweatshirt you don't care about keeping. When you begin to warm up, you can throw off the top layer without a second thought.

Mental Prep

As you arrive at the race venue, your nerves may be jumping. Don't panic—being nervous can be a good thing. It shows you respect the distance and you know that what you are doing is going to be tough. Instead of focusing on your nerves, however, spend time thinking about all the hard training you've put in, reassuring yourself that you are fit and ready to race. Remind yourself that training doesn't lie, and 2 + 2 = 4. Think of it as cautious confidence, which means being realistic about the difficulty of the race ahead, while also reminding yourself that your training has prepared you to handle it.

Accept that the task at hand is going to be hard and even hurt at times. This acknowledgment will arm you for when the going gets tough during the race. You knew it wasn't going to be a cakewalk. By preparing this way, you will have positive and motivating thoughts ready and waiting to help you endure. Indeed, as you are able to continue moving forward, despite the discomfort, you will likely be encouraged by your stamina and ability to persevere.

Race Protocol

Warming Up

You're about to run 26.2 miles. While a warm-up is a given for a faster, shorter race, you might wonder, do I really need to add more mileage to my marathon with a warm-up? The answer is yes: You should absolutely warm up. However, depending on goals, a warm-up will mean different things for different runners. It also depends on practicality. For instance, there's a lot more freedom to move around in a small race of a few hundred runners compared to a major marathon with 40,000 or more people. There are many reasons the marathon warm-up will differ from a warm-up prior to a shorter race. With a race like a 5K, you need to go from zero to fast in a very short time. That's not the case for a marathon. With that said, warming up your muscles remains important for both, but for one you are getting ready to drag race and the other you are getting ready to take a Sunday drive. What follows are some ideas about how you might approach the warm-up depending on your marathon goal time.

Sub 3:15 goal

For you, performance is key, so the pump has to be primed and ready to allow you to get into a pretty fast race pace and settle in. Ten minutes of light jogging, 5 minutes of dynamic stretching, and 5–10 minutes of strides should do the trick. Time this so you can hit the restrooms and get to the starting line on time.

3:16-4:00 goal

Consider the race itself. In a smaller race, you can do a light 10-minute jog and a dynamic warm-up (skip the strides) of 3–5 minutes and still get to the start line a few minutes before go time. In a bigger race, however, where you might be corralled for 20 minutes or longer, you may need to limit what you do for a warm-up. You can jog in place in the corral or do simple movements like squats. Also, if you know that you tend to go out too hard in races, cut back on your warm-up. Often, this inhibits the impulse to go out too fast, thus leading to a more desirable conservative start.

4:01-5:00+ goal

Those with later time goals will be lined up farther back in the corrals and thus be the last to cross the start line. If you are doing a large marathon, your walk to the start line may be lengthy enough to serve as a decent warm-up. In a smaller marathon, do a dynamic warm-up for 3–5 minutes, and then head to the corrals.

Race Strategy

First Miles (0-6)

The start can dictate how the rest of your race unfolds. The aim is to settle into your goal pace as soon as possible. You may well be dodging people in the first few miles, but remind yourself to stay calm. Don't make silly moves just to get around a slower group. Bide your time, run the tangents (the most direct route), and make your move when the opportunity arises.

Speaking of pace, what's the standard deviation in pace? The faster you are, the smaller that range is. For the 3:15 and faster crew, you are looking at a range of 5–10 seconds per mile either fast or slow, although I would prefer 5 seconds +/-. For 3:15–4:00 hours, give yourself a range of +/- 10 seconds. Beyond that, approximately 15 seconds fast or slow is your max deviation.

FUELING AT GO-TIME

When you are within 15 minutes of starting the race, take a gel (or whatever you plan to use for calories). This sets the precedent for your fueling plan and ensures that you keep your glycogen stores high for as long as possible. Don't worry about this causing an insulin response (i.e., blood sugar crash). You are going directly into exercise, so the energy will be used before your body tries to store it. For this to work, however, the gel must be taken within that 15-minute window.

However, be careful with these ranges. It doesn't mean that you can just run X seconds faster and all will be fine. That's not how it works. This deviation range simply means that you'll have some fast miles and some slow miles. If you can keep within that range, you'll average out to be pretty close to goal pace. But if you are consistently fast early on, which is easy to do, there's a good chance you'll pay dearly for it later on. Conversely, if you settle into a pace and it's slower, now is not the time to panic. It's early and there are ebbs and flows to the race. Don't try to force a faster pace. Stay relaxed and see if you naturally speed up. Sometimes it just takes a while to get the diesel fired up.

When it comes to nutrition and hydration, start early. Take your first gels/chews/drink about 30 minutes into the race. Remember, you took one 15 minutes before the race start, so at 30 minutes into the race, it's been about 45 minutes since your last caloric intake. A common mistake is deciding to pass on fluids and gels in the early miles because you're feeling good. The problem with that strategy is that you won't be able to make up for a deficit later on. Remember, that same pace will feel a lot harder at 20 miles, and at that point you aren't going to feel much like loading up on sports drinks and gels. Bottom line: Start hydrating and fueling early and you'll feel better later.

Middle Miles (7–20)

If you were able to settle into a rhythm early, this stretch will be easier on you mentally. It is a good point in the race to zone out and put your legs on autopilot. Remember: Pace, pace, pace. The time you spent doing tempo runs during your training will pay its dividends here.

Ideally, you'll be running among a pack of runners with similar goals, each sharing some of the work by helping to keep the pace or lead the pack. This will allow you to conserve some energy and zone out for big stretches. While it may seem counterintuitive to detach yourself from the moment, there's a method behind the madness. Intense focus for extended periods of time can be exhausting. In late stages of the race, when you really need your mental fortitude to overcome the physical degradation, you don't want to find yourself mentally fatigued. So put yourself in a position where you can use minimal mental energy to stay on task, knowing that the hard part is yet to come!

And remember, none of this will be possible if you don't stay on point with your nutrition and hydration. Your muscles aren't the only body parts that use carbs. The brain relies solely on carbs to fuel its fire. By staying hydrated and keeping your blood sugar up, you allow the muscle glycogen to be used where it needs to be and you keep your thoughts more focused and ready to dig deep. Your brain needs glycogen to function properly. If you are running low on glycogen, your thoughts will become foggy and it kicks open the door for poor decision-making. The clearer you can think, the easier it will be to convince yourself to persevere.

The Last 10K

You may have heard: "The marathon begins at 20 miles" or "Twenty miles is the halfway point in the marathon." These sentiments hold weight. But fortunately, everything we have talked about is setting you up to handle the toughest part of the marathon. There's no denying it: The last 6 miles will be a true test for you. Here are our top tips for not just completing that last 10K, but finishing strong:

Think small: Ideally, you get to 20 miles and, while you're feeling the effects of the miles, you remain confident that the big grizzly bear isn't going to hop on your back. Fatigue is certainly there, yet your thoughts remain crisp and you are still moving well. At this point in the race, maintaining mental sharpness is crucial. It allows you to gauge where you are at physically, to calculate splits, and have the fortitude to narrow your focus to the immediate task at hand. Think small. Instead of thinking about the fact that you have 6 miles to go, focus on the next 10 minutes or 1 mile or the next street light. When you get to that spot, hit reset and don't allow yourself to think beyond that. It's a great way to break a big chunk of distance up into manageable pieces.

Continue to take in carbs: Even if you just rinse your mouth out with sports drink, you can trick your brain into thinking it has had carbs and it will keep your intensity up. So if your stomach (or mind) is arguing against your taking anything in, keep that bit of trickery in mind.

Pick it up: If up to this point you have been conservative on pacing and are wondering when to pick up the pace, now is that time. That doesn't mean slamming your foot on the gas, but it does mean winding up your pace a bit. Even if you can't pick it up over the last 10K, you should be strong enough to minimize losses, rather than just hoping you put enough time in the bank. Hold steady and keep pushing forward one step at a time.

Race Day Checklist

- ☐ Shoes and socks
- ☐ Singlet and/or sports bra
- ☐ Shorts
- ☐ Water/sports drink
- ☐ Race number
- ☐ Timing chip
- ☐ Pins or race-number belt
- ☐ Energy gels
- ☐ Watch
- ☐ Sunglasses
- ☐ Hat/pony tail/elastic
- ☐ Lip balm and/or sunscreen
- ☐ Pre- and post-race clothes
- ☐ Towel
- ☐ Toilet paper or tissues
- ☐ Anti-chafing lubricant (Body Glide or petroleum jelly)
- ☐ Band-Aids to protect nipples (for the guys)
- ☐ Gloves/arm warmers
- ☐ Throwaway shirt and/or pants
- ☐ Money
- ☐ Equipment check bag containing post-race gear
- ☐ Directions to start and pre-race instructions

17

AFTER THE RACE

CONGRATULATIONS ON FINISHING THE MARATHON! After all that hard work, you may be wondering what's next. For the Hansons-Brooks Distance Project elite team, two weeks of no running is the cardinal rule following a marathon. The same goes for you. Regardless of whether you met your goals or fell short, you need to take a couple weeks of downtime. When you cross that finish line, you're like a racecar driver hoping that there's just enough fuel to get the car past the checkered flags. While you'll be fueling and hydrating throughout your race, there is no way to keep your stores topped off. By the time the finish line is in sight, you're likely running on empty. Taking a break from running after the marathon is important because it gives your body sufficient time to bring glycogen and hydration levels back to normal.

But do you really need two whole weeks off? In short, yes. Your body goes through a lot during the marathon, which makes proper recovery vital. To understand the process, let's look closer at the typical aches and fatigue a runner feels after a marathon. Contrary to popular belief, your post-race pain or discomfort is *not* caused by lactic acid overflowing your bloodstream. You weren't running hard enough to produce massive amounts of lactic acid, and what you were producing was recycled in the liver and turned back into glucose. Anything that was in your bloodstream was gone within several minutes of finishing.

What then are the real culprits of marathon fatigue? As discussed earlier in the book, we know we become dehydrated and glycogen-depleted during the race. Another factor is the very real damage done to our muscle fibers while running 26.2. While physical responses to a marathon are highly individual, most runners will have at least light damage on a cellular level, and therefore need to allow for muscle glycogen replenishment for several days to a week.

This step-by-step guide details how to handle the minutes, hours, days, and weeks post-marathon.

Immediately Post-Race

Take a few moments after your race to revel in the fact that you took your body to the edge and made it to the finish. No matter what the clock says, as long as you gave the race your best shot, you can count your marathon a success. Allow yourself to be proud of this major accomplishment! Along with those positive feelings will most certainly come soreness and exhaustion. Many seasoned runners report standing in the finishing chute after their first marathon and thinking, "There is absolutely no way I will ever do that again." And then they go on to do several more. Yes, marathons can hurt, but after that first race, many runners are hooked.

The First 30 Minutes

While you may wince at the thought of eating, try to consume some calories right away. It doesn't really matter what it is; in fact, you can pretty much eat anything you are craving. Whether it is a bowl of chicken broth, a Coke, or chocolate chip cookies, at this point what is important are the calories, not the source from which they are coming. This is a good thing because you usually can't be picky when it comes to finish-line fare. Whatever they are offering, take it. Since you have depleted nearly all of your available muscle and liver glycogen, your body will bounce back far sooner if you eat now. What's more, your blood glucose is low, you're dehydrated, and you have only a few remaining electrolytes. The faster you start replacing these nutrients, the sooner you'll be back to feeling normal. The window of optimal recovery time is brief, so take advantage of the goodies in the finish area during those first 30 minutes after the race.

The First 2 Hours

Once you gather your hardware and snacks, leave the finish area and find your family and friends. As long as you have had something to eat and drink, you don't need to worry about consuming a full meal until your stomach settles down. Go back to your hotel room or home, get cleaned up, and put on comfortable clothes. By that point you may be ready for a full meal. Focus on taking in a high percentage of carbohydrates to replace that lost glycogen. If you still don't feel quite ready for a feast, steadily consume calories to get in a good amount over time. Nutritious snacks will help get your system back on track. Fruits, vegetables, and whole grains are great options, along with water, fruit juice, or sports drinks.

The Rest of the Day

Continue to hydrate and replace calories as desired. Put your feet up and relax for a few hours; you earned it. Although you may feel stiff and tired, make it a point to get up and walk around later in the evening to loosen up your legs. This can help with the soreness that will likely set in by the following morning.

WHAT CAN I DO DURING DOWNTIME?

- Rest, refuel, and rehydrate.
- Lay off heavy stretching as this will actually reduce blood flow.
- Take a few days off from any exercise, but then slowly add in low-impact crosstraining. This can improve recovery rates by increasing blood flow.

The Next 3–5 Days

Mobility may be tricky for the next few days. Your first steps out of bed the following morning will be labored, and walking up and down stairs may seem a challenge akin to climbing Mount Everest. From elites to weekend warriors, no one escapes a marathon without at least a little soreness. Besides the glycogen depletion, the structural integrity of the muscles has been compromised, so don't plan any big outings right after the marathon.

Don't run at all during this period. Remember, taking a break from running is extremely beneficial to your body. Some runners fall into a cycle of jumping right back into mileage just a few days after the marathon, often leaving their legs feeling stale a month or two down the line. Rest now, so that you can recover completely. Use this time to catch up on the things that took a backseat during training, and enjoy the break. If you feel like you must do something, go for light walks.

The Next 2 Weeks

Many runners dislike taking time off from running, worried they might lose precious fitness. It's important, however, to understand how a break fits into the bigger picture of training. Planned time off can prevent a forced break down the line due to injury or overtraining. You are better off allowing yourself some time off now, even though it may feel like a major deviation from the routine you established over the past few months. You can take the entire two weeks away from exercise altogether. It's also OK to incorporate some cross-training, provided that it's not too intense. A light resistance training program or a cycling regimen are reasonable options. Crosstraining helps to maintain the routine you worked so hard to build, making it easier to resume running again. Just refrain from running for these two weeks to let your body completely recover before getting out and pounding the pavement again.

2 Weeks Post-Marathon

Following your two-week rest, feel free to start running again. Approach your return conservatively, however. Some runners want to begin planning their next race before they are even two weeks out from the marathon. While it is excellent to have goals and we applaud the desire to continue training, remember to be flexible with your plans. For newbies and veterans alike, it is important to wait and see how your individual recovery goes in order to avoid the pitfalls of rushing back to hard training too soon.

Once you have established that you're fully recovered and ready to get back into a running routine, start small, with an easy running regimen. Those first few runs may feel more difficult than usual. Don't worry; you haven't lost as much ground as you think. Two weeks off will have decreased your fitness by about 5 percent, a small number in the training cycle.

Start with 30 minutes of jogging every other day. The first week might look like the table on p. 282.

Resistance training can also be resumed, two or three times each week. This should be done on days that you will not be doing SOS workouts in the upcoming weeks, allowing you to get into a routine. For example, if you know that in the future you'll be doing SOS workouts on Tuesday, Thursday, and Sunday, establish your resistance-training days on Monday, Wednesday,

TABLE 17.1 **FIRST WEEK BACK TO RUNNING**

Monday	20–30 min. of slow running
Tuesday	Off (crosstrain/resistance training)
Wednesday	25–30 min. of slow running
Thursday	Off (same as Tuesday)
Friday	30 min. of slow running
Saturday	Off (same as Tuesday)
Sunday	30 min. of slow running

and/or Friday. By starting the regimen at this time, you can build running-specific strength without doing a single workout for several weeks.

After following the aforementioned mileage for the first week back to training, you might consider bringing things up a notch for the second week, although it should still all be easy mileage. If you are feeling refreshed and looking forward to getting back on track, add a bit of mileage. A beginner should add two days with 30-minute runs, bringing the weekly total to five days of 30-minute runs each. More advanced runners can add time to each of their running days, aiming for 45–60 minutes of easy running, six days a week. If you are still feeling sore and tired, however, don't hesitate to give yourself another week to linger at lower mileage and let your body and mind recover.

4–6 Weeks Post-Marathon

After those first two weeks of easy running, spend the next two weeks building mileage, allowing for a slow return back up to your typical training volume. Most runners will run their highest mileage during marathon training, so at this point there is no need to get that high until you are certain what your next goals are. Rather, maintain a base of 50–60 percent of what your peak mileage was. So, if you peaked at 45 miles per week during marathon training, try running 20–25 miles per week for a few weeks. You'll probably find this much more comfortable than when you started marathon training several months ago. It also sets you up to go in any direction you want to go, whether it's fitness running or an ultra marathon. You now have a foundation to build any training block you want.

The Great Beyond

The question at this point is where to go from here. Many runners feel they need to get right back into marathon training, although this isn't the optimal choice for a lot of runners. At Hansons, we have a rule known as the "3–2 rule." This simply means three marathons every two years, and ideally these are not back-to-back.

For brand-new runners who went zero to 26.2, you might want to take a step back and focus on a new goal of a shorter distance. When you are ready to start an organized training block, consider a 10–12 week training segment for the 5K and then the 10K distance. After that, build on that speed, as well as on your endurance, and aim your sights on a new marathon goal in the next year or so.

For more experienced runners, it may be better not to wait as long before training for another marathon. You will be better served training for a shorter race for 10–12 weeks, then reaping the new speed and the residual strength lingering from your marathon training and going after another one. If you ran a fall marathon, for example, you could train for a short race over the winter (such as a local turkey trot), and then start training for a spring marathon at the start of the new year.

Assessing Race Success and Determining Future Directions

Many runners run their first marathon, and then have a desire to level up with a more challenging training plan for their next 26.2. When considering a program for your next marathon, take all factors into consideration. The marathon has a steep learning curve. If you followed a schedule that felt slightly too tough the first time around, you may be able to repeat that same schedule a year down the road and have it be completely manageable, and with better end results. Or, you may have trained hard and fallen short. The answer isn't then to train harder to achieve the goal. Chances are, you were in a schedule that was too aggressive for your ability at that time. Don't be afraid to take a step back into a schedule that is more manageable for your current fitness.

Every training cycle, regardless of the race-day result, contains value for an athlete. Identifying patterns of success and failure is crucial to long-term success. Hopefully, race day brings with it a payout for your hard work, but sometimes it doesn't. Either way, it is important to review the training cycle as a whole and look for the components that increased fitness and those that inhibited it. Useful questions to ask yourself after a training cycle include:

- Was I able to complete all of the training as scheduled? If not, did I run more than scheduled or less?

- Was I able to hit all the prescribed workout paces? If not, were there specific workout types that gave me trouble?

- Did I run any of the workouts, easy days, or long runs faster than prescribed?

- Was this training cycle at a higher level of weekly mileage than usual? Higher than I've ever done?

> Was the goal pace faster than I've ever run?
> Was goal pace too aggressive?

> Were my goals appropriate relative to recent performances and fitness?

> What was my pre-race routine like compared to past cycles?

> How well did I execute my race plan? Did I start too fast? Too slow?

> Did I have people to race? Was the crowd support good?

> What was going on in my life during this training cycle?

> Did I get sick during this training cycle?

> Was I dealing with any injuries this training cycle?

> What was my sleep like this training cycle?

> What was the weather like this training cycle?
> Did I adjust for weather?

The goal is to look for parameters that correlate with success and failure. From there, work to incorporate those associated with success and mindfully eliminate or adjust those that seem to factor in failure. Teasing apart the factors related to both will allow you to progress through higher levels of fitness more quickly than those who do not do so.

Once you've identified some success and failure factors, where do you go next? After your important and well-deserved downtime, thoughtfully consider your options. Need help deciding? Check out the decision tree in Figure 17.1.

FIGURE 17.1 **DECISION TREE**

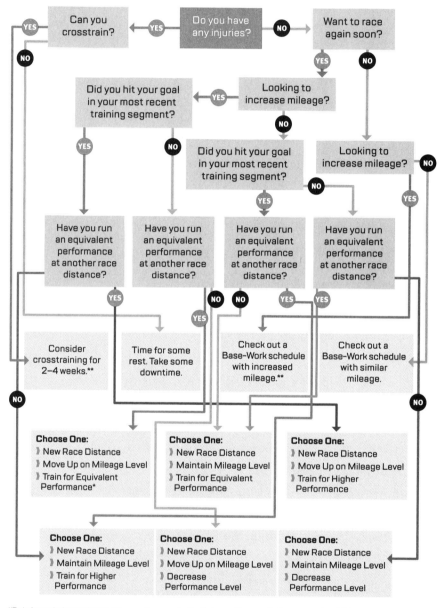

*"Train for equivalent performance" means focus on shorter distances. For example, if you want to break 3 hours in the marathon but haven't broken 1:30 in the half-marathon, consider a training cycle to work on bringing your half-marathon time down to an equivalent 3-hour marathon performance before going back to attempt that marathon goal time.

**The Hansons base-building and crosstraining programs can be found at www.hansonscoachingservices.com.

Acknowledgments

People often give me a funny look when they realize my last name is not Hanson. I get it; why am I writing the books if it's Kevin and Keith Hanson's work? To be honest, that is a very legitimate question. I am beyond blessed that the brothers allow me to be the torchbearer for their training methods. In 2004 they took a big chance on an average runner from Central Michigan University and then took another big chance on the same young adult in 2011. I am forever thankful to them for giving me two big opportunities in my life.

My wife has been the guinea pig for a few of my schedule adjustments to the classic Hansons marathon plans. For the most part they have worked, so we kept moving forward with them. All of your success hinges on her! I am mostly kidding, except I really did try a lot of the adjustments with her. My family is a big part of why I reluctantly keep writing books. I am a terrible writer!

To all my coaches at Hansons Coaching Services. Corey Kubatzky, Mike Morgan, Melissa Johnson-White, Katie Kellner, Josh Eberly, and Dani Filipek. All these coaches have carried the torch well, freed up my responsibilities, and given me an opportunity to continue to spread the Hanson message.

This book wouldn't be possible if it weren't for all the athletes who trust us with their training. From the athletes we coach individually to our incredibly active

Facebook group for HMM users, you have all provided such great insight into the needs of the marathoner. While I think we taught you about accomplishing more than you thought you could, you gave us great insight into training, preparation, and goals of today's marathoners. Most of you realized you want to run faster, you just needed someone to teach you how to do it. That was the primary inspiration for this book.

Index

Page numbers followed by *t* and *f* refer to tables and figures.

About the Authors

Luke Humphrey began running track in middle school and hasn't slowed down since. After several all-state performances in high school, Luke ran for Central Michigan University from 1999 to 2004. There he was a member of several NCAA Division I top-25 cross-country teams, including a 9th place team in 2002. In fall of 2004 Luke competed in his first marathon at the LaSalle Bank Chicago Marathon for the Hansons-Brooks Distance  Project. He ran a debut time of 2:18:46 and was 18th overall. Since then Luke has gone on to finish 11th in the 2006 Boston Marathon, 11th in the 2008 ING New York City Marathon, and 12th in the 2010 Bank of America Chicago Marathon and has also qualified for three U.S. Olympic Trials for the marathon (2008, 2012, and 2016). Luke holds a personal best of 2:14:38 in the marathon. He has a B.A.A. in exercise science from Central Michigan University and an M.S. in exercise science from Oakland University. Luke began Hansons Coaching Services in May 2006 to help runners of all abilities reach their running goals. He and his wife, Nicole, have a daughter, Josephine.

Keith and Kevin Hanson are cofounders of the Hansons-Brooks Distance Project, together coaching the Olympic development team to victories on national and international stages. They also co-own the Hansons Running Shops and avidly support, build, and encourage the running community, coaching hundreds of local runners to their first or 100th marathon.